FANS
Not Customers

How to Create Growth in a No Growth World

VERNON HILL

with **Bob Andelman**

PROFILE BOOKS

First published in Great Britain in 2012 by
Profile Books Ltd
3A Exmouth House
Pine Street
Exmouth Market
London EC1R OJH
www.profilebooks.com

1 3 5 7 9 10 8 6 4 2

Typeset in Minion by MacGuru Ltd
info@macguru.org.uk

Printed in the United States

A CIP catalogue record for this book is available from the British Library.

ISBN 978 1 78125 111 9
e-ISBN 978 1 84765 956 9

FANS
Not Customers

What People Are Saying About Vernon Hill

"Vernon reinvented American retail banking. His focus on service created a true growth retailer. No one else has grown an American bank internally at 25 percent per year for 30-plus years. *No one.*

"I think Shirley, Vernon's wife, was the secret weapon of Commerce Bank and is exactly that now at Metro Bank. She is the keeper of the brand, produces design as a competitive weapon, and enforces the culture."

Tom Brown, founder, BankStocks.com

"Vernon told me that the whole point of the company is that it's a *symphony*. The performance works because everything works in concert and so, if you don't buy it in its entirety, you can't ever get it to work for you. Vernon's competition over the years simply refused to learn from Commerce Bank."

William C. Taylor, author, *Mavericks At Work*

"I was at the opening of the first branch of Metro Bank in London. It was incredible. Incredible! It's Commerce—and even better!"

Meredith Whitney, founder, Meredith Whitney
Advisory Group LLC

To our loyal team members, investors and customers.

To my partners, John Silvestri, Steve Lewis, John Scardapane, Chris and Natasha Ashton, Gary Nalbandian, and Craig Donaldson for their dedication, loyalty and support.

And to my beloved wife and life partner Shirley, with whom I have shared an incredibly rewarding life's journey, memorable travels, vision of the future and success at work and at home.

Contents

Foreword

Tom Peters

Writing this foreword is easy—and impossible. The "easy option": Just include every page of the book in my bit here. That is, I didn't find *anything* not worth reading, in fact ingesting, nary a "non-Wow" in sight. Writing a foreword to this book is impossible: There is so much I want to say and say in detail—and commend.

No kidding, this is the toughest foreword I've done, because I won't know where to stop, and want to say so much more than space permits. Such as:

- The story of Commerce Bank and NOW Metro Bank is virtually one of a kind—they do so damn much right.
- The bank works, absurdly well, from a P&L standpoint. Hence, Doing the right stuff = Doing the profitable stuff.
- You can make money, lots of, off a "customer service model"—there are skeptics galore. ("Fools," I call them. Sorry.) (Of course there is a problem, and a big one: You can lose your shirt with a "SORT OF good service" approach—which costs a ton and is not memorable.)
- The bank takes on the regnant business model—and clobbers it. They want me in the branch (and WHAT A

BRANCH!—more later) dealing with their folks face-to-face, not out of sight at the ATM or on the web.

- "Cost cutting is a death spiral"—that sweet music is worth the price of admission all by itself, to me—it's long been my religion. Commerce and Metro tell us there are two choices for "doing business": (1) cost-cut your way to prosperity; or (2) spend your way to prosperity. And the answer is: There is indeed an ALMOST SUREFIRE answer: spend!

- Spend: *Over*-invest in people. *Over*-invest in facilities. What could be more obvious? (And so rarely practiced by even our so-called "best" organizations—especially in banking.)

- These guys want—*desperately* almost—to shower me with attention. (Darn close to "love and affection"—yes a b-a-n-k.)

- And the "me" is everyone! Forget the "high net worth customer." Forget the "80–20 rule": Metro wants us all!

- They want to make "AMAZE," "AMAZE-ing," "AMAZE-ness" as normal as breathing—and they're happy to use that "hot" word.

- These "bankers" not only want me—but they want my dog!

- They want me darn near "24/7"—the "7" for sure and close to the 24.

- They are—yes, a "bank"—colorful. They pig out on Red and BlueRed and Blue. Red and blue. And then more … red and blue.

- I'm a "design nut"—I think design matters, a lot and everywhere—JUST LOOK AT APPLE. "Cool design" in a "bank"—yup, top marks on that one too. (The word "matchless" comes to mind.)

- Back to the "business model"—they are foursquare champions of Organic Growth. (I consider myself Public

Enemy Number One of the "marriage of dinosaurs," otherwise known as 90 PERCENT OF mega-mergers.) (Small, perfectly targeted acquisitions are okay; they don't screw up the culture. Yikes, I've been preaching this to deaf ears for 25 years.)

- Back to the business model redux: these guys believe that people will pay a little more (or accept a slightly smaller return) in recompense for knock-your-socks-off-all-the-time service.
- Commerce believed they could "make it in Manhattan"— and did they ever; "instant success" was just that.
- Commerce "proved it," not only with profit but also with tiptop awards from the likes of J.D. Power. (And some amazing testimonials from tough cookies, scattered throughout the book.)
- They believe you can go for fast growth—and keep the spirit intact.
- "They" hate-hate-hate bureaucracy. So do I! (You'll learn about Red Buttons that extinguish stupid rules in good time—I really don't want to spoil the story.)
- They love training—call it what it is, "indoctrination" or "boot camp" for the company "culture."
- They groove on the word "Yes" (to customer requests) and treat "No" as if it were a four-letter word, not a mere two. Yes = Of course we can, just watch us. "No" = Mortal sin, not in our vocabulary.
- Customer service at this level costs money (learn inside about the expensive change machines, not to mention the cost of dog biscuits and balloons); and Metro spends that money.
- If you're going to give great service to your customers, then you've got to put employees "MORE first"—the "Thanks for

the good work" parties are concocted with the brakes off.

- *"Kaizen"* is fine—do stuff a little better. But the Commerce and Metro story is not about "a little better"—it's about in-your-face-over-the-top-visible-all-the-time better.

Believe it or not, these 24 bullet points amount to no more than scratching the surface of the surface, offering you the tiniest of hors d'oeuvres. As I said, only going "ditto" to the whole book would do the whole book justice.

This is a bit weird: Why in the hell would Metro Bank give away its secrets in such startling detail? Well, it's fun to tell a great tale. But I'll tell you something else—this book is darn near uncopyable. (The authors may balk at that—tough.) Why? Because it requires a level of sustaining commitment that is stratospheric. No doubt one can pick up "a tip or two"—it won't hurt and it will probably help. But to be able to support such a contrarian model in the face of Monster Competitors means aiming for and delivering on over and over and over what my marketing guru pal, Doug Hall, calls "Dramatic Difference." What Vernon Hill calls "AMAZE"—day in and day out (remember, damn near 24/7).

I'd add one or two more things: The book works for a woman starting a one-person accountancy. Or for a CEO of BigCo trying to stand out in a crowded market. It does not work for the faint of heart—to be this different takes guts, and takes equal devotion to "the vision thing" *and* "the execution thing"!

There is a Hall of Fame, or at least my Hall of Fame, of the Customer Service Kings. It includes the likes of: Starbucks, Whole Foods Market, Four Seasons hotels, Cirque du Soleil, London Drug in western and central Canada. And Gary Drug, on Charles Street in Boston—a block from my home. And, the equal of any: Vernon Hill's Commerce Bank and Metro Bank.

Way to go Commerce—and Metro!

To readers:

- Enjoy!
- Learn!
- Steal!
- Implement!

And: Think seriously, very very seriously, if you are ready to commit to and to create and to adhere to a "culture" that supports this "absurd" level of service. I'D NEVER MAKE A "GUARANTEE"—LIFE IS TOO COMPLEX FOR THAT. BUT I WOULD BET A PRETTY PENNY THAT MANY A PRETTY PENNY WILL BE YOURS IF YOU FOLLOW SOME CLOSE KIN TO THIS APPROACH.

Tom Peters, author or co-author of many international best-sellers on business and management, most notably *In Search of Excellence*, which one survey rated the "greatest business book of all time".

Welcome!

Despite appearances to the contrary, this is not a book about banking.

Really, it's not.

Does your bank open early, close late and welcome you seven days a week?

Does it let one person tell you yes, but require at least two to say no?

Does it invite your dog inside for a treat?

Does it educate and entertain your children?

Does it inspire fans, not customers?

That doesn't sound like any bank I know. Except Metro Bank, the one I co-founded in London in 2010.

Which brings me back to my original point: This is *not* a book about banking.

Metro Bank doesn't have branches; it has stores. It doesn't have employees; it has team members. It doesn't chain its pens to desks so customers can't walk away with them; it gives out millions of pens and encourages customers and non-customers alike to take them home and share them with friends.

And I can't emphasize this point enough: *fans*, not customers.

This book is packed with learnable lessons from the

Commerce Bank and Metro Bank experiences in the United States and United Kingdom, respectively. You'll even find them collected in a convenient appendix at the end. These are the immutable truths that we discovered along our journey. I hope they help you rethink your own business in the future.

Don't approach this book the way you would the story of some unsexy, boring bank. We compete with them, but we're not *of* them. We represent a retail experience you won't soon forget—and we think *your* business should, too.

This is a book about exploiting your potential as a company or employee. Whatever describes you, I think that you'll find ideas and methods in the pages that follow that will make you a greater, more valuable asset to yourself and your company.

To my fellow entrepreneurs, recognize and grasp your opportunities as they present themselves; learn how you can deliver value, differentiation, and improvement. I believe in: the importance of branding; that hope is not a plan; that no one needs a "Me, Too" anything; and that value creators are wealth creators.

Metro is definitely not your grandfather's idea of a bank.

And this is definitely not a book about banking.

Vernon Hill
London
September 2012

Introduction: Start-Ups and Upstarts

The best way to predict the future is to invent it.

Alan Kay, co-creator of laptop computing and graphic user interfaces, and the man whose work directly influenced the creation of Apple's Macintosh computer

Great customer-focused retail brands are few and far between:

- Apple
- Four Seasons Hotels and Resorts
- John Lewis
- IKEA
- Amazon
- Commerce Bank and Petplan in the US, and now Metro Bank in London

My life's focus has been on creating great brands and great companies. In this book, I will share my philosophy of business and wealth creation. You'll learn how to build companies that have value to customers, investors and yourself. And if you're a team member of one of our own businesses, including Metro Bank and Petplan, you'll learn exactly what is expected of you and how to chart a path of growth, accomplishment and success.

With me, every conversation about building a great brand, generating wealth and creating fans, starts with three primary elements:

Differentiated *Model* +
Pervasive *Culture* +
Fanatical *Execution* =
FANS not customers

It's a customer service-centric business model that I believe can be applied to any business, in any industry.

Steve Jobs, co-founder of Apple, believed in the highest possible levels of customer service but not necessarily in giving the customer what he thinks he wants. He told biographer Walter Isaacson, author of the 2011 bestseller *Steve Jobs*:

> Some people say, "Give the customers what they want." But that's not my approach. Our job is to figure out what they're going to want before they do. I think Henry Ford once said, "If I'd asked customers what they wanted, they would have told me, 'A faster horse.'" People don't know what they want until you show it to them. That's why I never rely on market research. Our task is to read things that are not yet on the page.

Jobs ignored market research and never ordered it. And I never have, either. He had an innate ability to see beyond what market research could tell us. If you're inventing the future, what is market research going to tell you?

*

I founded Commerce Bank in southern New Jersey in 1973.

When we took the concept into Manhattan 28 years later, the financial press saw red. How could a little bank from New Jersey compete in the Big Apple? Reporters and columnists that failed to do their homework didn't realize that we had already established and proven a unique customer model, and exactly the same thing happened more recently as we introduced Metro Bank to London in 2010.

How could this no-name, no-brand new bank compete with the London high street banks? All the market research said it couldn't. It said the British wouldn't switch banks under any circumstances. But we were about to deliver something that market research couldn't measure, a level of service that people couldn't compare with anything they previously experienced: a unique retail experience. We arrived and gave people something that they didn't know existed.

In May 2000, Apple's value was one-twentieth of Microsoft's. In August 2012, Apple became the most valuable company in history. The iPhone and the iPad were not lucky flukes. They were the natural result of the progression Jobs spent his life perfecting.

No matter how much a company brags about itself, customers know the truth. They may buy a Windows PC or an Android mobile phone because that's what their company requires, but they're nowhere near as happy as the Apple user who is literally a fan of the manufacturer. John Lewis in Britain, IKEA, Carrefour, Four Seasons, and Starbucks, worldwide, similarly prosper by redefining customer service.

How do I know that Commerce Bank (and now Metro Bank) created *FANS not customers*? I could say it was the intense loyalty that developed around the brand. Or I could let Tom Petro, senior vice president of J.D. Power and Associates, a leading customer service research firm, do the talking for me:

> Commerce applied out-of-the-box thinking to what is
> normally a fairly buttoned-up business. What Commerce

has done so well is to figure out what their niche is. With Commerce, it's about friendly service and convenience, kind of the everyman's bank ... According to the voice of the customer that J.D. Power is hearing, Commerce just does a great, great job and stands out among the crowd.

Fans tell their friends about you. They join your team. At family and friends' barbecues, they tell everyone about something magnificent your employees did for them, above and beyond the call of duty. They don't patronize you, they *become* you.

The premise of this book is to demonstrate how Metro Bank and Petplan employees build fantastic value by creating fans. It's the *Good to Great* story with real-life examples from someone who lived them.

Great businesses attract new customers, retain these customers and watch as happy customers become fans and recommend their family and friends: *FANS not customers*!

*

One more thing about this book and our businesses in general: I didn't do any of this alone.

In 1973, besides opening the doors at Commerce Bank, I married my wife, Shirley, on December 22. A graduate of the Pratt Institute in Brooklyn, she subsequently founded her own design firm, InterArch, and established a unique ability to unite architecture, design and brand building. With Shirley by my side, design is a major competitive weapon—one every entrepreneur should pursue.

Over the years, Shirley and I have been partners in creating the design and executing the unique brands and facilities of Metro Bank, Petplan and Commerce Bank. She and her team created and executed the look and brand at Commerce, and she is a critical element in the look and the feel of our latest brands as well.

Shirley's role was originally to interpret, preserve and enhance the brands as well as create a unique exterior architecture and interior design. I developed the model and set the standards for Commerce Bank: "America's Most Convenient Bank." When I said things such as "the world doesn't need another 'Me, Too' anything," Shirley and the staff of InterArch took a commoditized business and turned it into a retail brand. They added emotion, commercial appeal, and fun.

One of the greatest examples of her work can be found in Metro Bank's Magic Money Machines, the free to use coin counting devices in every Metro Bank lobby. Imagine the moment the manufacturer rolled the prototype black boxes—measuring 36 × 24 × 24 inches, which, unvarnished, look like small refrigerators—into her office. Her job? Make it "AMAZE!" customers.

Making these companies soar is also about the development of environments, the attention to detail, and great respect for the creative aspects. Shirley gives our facilities the energy and positive vibe that customers love. She knows me and the Metro Bank and Petplan businesses better than anyone else could after four decades on the job together; with her professional skills, who could I possibly trust more to get it right?

I believe that great design is a pillar of great *companies*, and when you go in our stores, you will be AMAZEd, too.

We've also discovered a new partner in London in the person of Metro Bank's CEO, Craig Donaldson. You'll learn more about him later; he is a person who lives and breathes the Metro Bank culture. Making the model and brand grow in the UK is a personal quest for him because this is his country and Metro Bank is his bank. It's the application of our business tenets, for which he has spent his entire career searching.

In these pages, I shall describe and expand upon our beliefs and experiences. I believe you have unlimited potential to be all you can be. Your company—large or small—needs you to succeed and grow. You have the potential to be a star.

To entrepreneurs, the future is yours. Each of you has unique talents, and if you are lucky enough to match these talents with your vocation, your future is also unlimited.

No one needs a "Me, Too" business or a "Me, Too" team member. You and your business need to add value, everywhere, every day.

Good luck in creating your own *FANS NOT CUSTOMERS*!

Part 1

Two Banks, Two Continents: A World of Lessons

1

Metro: A New Bank for a New Century

> **Dream more than others think practical. Expect more than others think possible. Care more than others think wise.**
>
> Howard Schultz, founder, Starbucks

Several days after my departure from Commerce Bank in the US, my Metro Bank UK co-founder, Anthony Thomson, invited me to help him break through the century-old resistance of Britain's financial environment and build the country's first newly authorized retail bank in generations. The experience has been nothing short of exhilarating.

When we opened our doors to the public in July 2010, Metro Bank became the first new London high street bank in over 100 years. With one enormously successful grand opening, we changed the course of business for generations to come.

Metro Bank employs the bank model and culture that I developed and that was an unparalleled success in the US for more than three decades. Now we have exported it to the UK. We plan to have 200 offices in Greater London by 2020 and at least 5,000 team members and £25 billion in deposits. We're going to Apple-ize the banking world in Britain, particularly in Greater London.

We offer banking focused on the customer through

unparalleled levels of service and convenience. With our unique, customer-focused business we reinvent the rules of retail banking, making every effort to remove all stupid bank rules from our services to offer simpler and more convenient banking to our fans. Our stores (a term we prefer to "bank branches" because there is nothing traditional about our sites) are open seven days a week, which demonstrates our commitment to customers that we're open for *their* convenience, not ours. And our call centers never close, with live team members answering customer questions and solving problems 24/7.

Metro Bank is a true growth company—from our model to our culture to our investment philosophy. Our deposit growth comes from two areas: comparable store deposit growth from our current store base, and new stores.

Comparable store growth is the core of any great retailer. If you cannot grow your existing stores, you do not deserve to expand. Comparable store growth has proven to be the only reliable predictor of new store success.

To Metro Bank, being a power retailer means more than serving just the consumer market. We believe in delivering a unique, differentiating, value-added customer experience to every segment we serve, including consumer, commercial and governmental.

In our world, Metro Bank is nothing like a bank at all. It has "bank" in its name, but that's about it.

In all our stores you'll encounter face-to-face service with no requirement to book an appointment to discuss your banking needs. We instantly open your new personal and/or business account—often in 15 minutes—and offer card and cheque printers on site so you can walk away with everything you need to start using your account immediately. Call us on the phone and you'll receive unparalleled service from a live person, 24 hours a day, 7 days a week, 365 days a year. We aim to exceed the expectations of our customers every day.

The day we opened the first Metro Bank store in London, the place was a complete mob scene, not unlike the arrival of the first Apple store in Beijing in 2012. The excitement was broadcast live on BBC One for three hours—that's right, people in the act of opening new current and savings accounts captivated an entire nation. It was a scene of extraordinary excitement and, frankly, a little pandemonium.

*

You could say that the world didn't need another bank, but we always said that what the world didn't need was another "Me, Too" bank. What the UK needed pretty badly in banking was something it lacked: outstanding customer service and convenience.

As construction proceeded apace, we were told by "the experts" that our colors were too bright and we were far too brash, that "Love Your Bank At Last" was far too in-your-face, that our "Dogs Rule" would never work, and as for "Kids Rock," well, we shouldn't say "rock" about kids. We were told by experts, "You should use pastels, maybe a light green and a soft yellow."

We dismissed all this misbegotten advice. Something that propelled our confidence was the early hiring of Craig Donaldson, our CEO. He is responsible for providing executive leadership to the bank's already 500-strong team. He is charged with guiding the bank's evolution from fresh, new entrant in retail banking to trusted financial services partner to millions of British customers.

From helping define Metro Bank's brand values, to hiring its inaugural employees and ensuring that the bank's staff deliver daily customer delight, Craig has been instrumental to Metro Bank from day one. His previous roles included managing director of retail products at RBS, as well as senior roles with Barclays and HBOS.

But despite his credentials, Craig is as unlike a typical British banker as anyone I've ever met. He spent most of his career railing against the stuffy London high street habits of inconvenient bank hours, lousy customer service and countless stupid rules.

Furthermore, Craig studied the Commerce Bank model at Harvard Business School in Boston and experienced it in action in the mid-2000s. He knew the British banking business could be better than it was, and after seeing Commerce create *FANS not customers*, he grew even more frustrated with business as usual back at home.

"I was probably seen as the guy who always railed against it from the inside," Craig told me. "I always knew this could work. What's not to like about service and convenience? But it could only be created from scratch."

When we brought Metro Bank to the UK, Craig was a natural to lead the revolution.

*

Almost every media report on the opening of the first Metro Bank—and almost every store we've opened since then—likened the look of our premises to an expensive hotel lobby or a casino.

Once you walk inside one of our stores, you know life is different because it doesn't at all resemble the typical British banking experience. Many British banks commit a full third of their retail space to ATMs because they don't want customers to talk to customer service representatives. We, on the other hand, want customers inside our stores, "safe, dry, and free." We want them on hand to see and enjoy the bank.

One day it was raining at the new Holborn store and we looked across the street and saw 20 people queuing up, in the rain, waiting to use an ATM outside a Sainsbury's supermarket.

It made us crazy seeing their inconvenience when we had four ATMs indoors. We marched across the street with raincoats and umbrellas and escorted them back to our dry environs.

*

No model works without team members who believe in it and fundamentally execute it. We have recruited hundreds of team members—and will recruit thousands more in the future—and they have seen the magic of a unique culture executing the right model.

In the retail business there are companies that grow rapidly. They attract because they create excitement. People want to get a thrill out of patronizing your business, whether it's a bank, a retail store or even a pet insurance company.

Metro Bank is on its way toward creating fans and redefining British banking. And I can't wait to tell you how we do it.

2

Commerce Bank: Early Days, Winning Ways

I was an overnight success all right, but 30 years is a long, long night.

Ray Kroc, McDonald's

You must believe in your model.

I think that making money is the result, not the objective, of what you do. I was always fascinated with business models— what's good and what's bad and why some succeed and others fail. And you often learn more from the ones that fail. What's the differentiator? Why does one succeed and another fail?

At one time in the US, McDonald's, Burger King and Burger Chef were all about the same size, and Burger Chef, which was owned by General Foods, had the deepest pockets. Yet Burger Chef was wiped off the face of the earth, and Burger King has been a weak second ever since. What is it about McDonald's that allowed it to come from a position of equal in the pack to be the dominant player? We see that in lots of business categories. What's the differentiator? Certainly, it's the people who manage a business, but it's always more than that.

It's something about the model that is different.

*

Commerce Bank opened its doors on June 29, 1973, in Marlton, New Jersey. It was a modest start, with just nine employees and plenty of doubters, but by 2007, it was a major American bank, growing at 25 percent per year. It went from being one of 24,000 community banks to being a regional powerhouse with a reputation for service on a par with McDonald's, John Lewis, Apple and Starbucks.

Over 34 years, Shirley and I and a dedicated team of professionals built Commerce Bank from one location in southern New Jersey to 440 stores in six states with $50 billion in assets and $8 billion in market capitalization.

It proved to be a great investment. While the better-known Starbucks stores netted $75,000 per unit at the dizzying height of their popularity, a Commerce store netted $1 million on average to the bottom line. Anyone who invested $10,000 in Commerce Bank from the start, in 1973, would have seen their investment grow in value to $4.7 million in 2007. That's a 470 times increase, a 23 percent stock return compounded for 30 years.

We knew what we wanted to be, and we knew what we didn't want to be, and those lines just didn't cross. We were the attack model. What separated us was the consistency in what we do and the discipline to reinvent retail banking.

*

I am the oldest of six children. I grew up in Vienna, Virginia, a suburb of Washington, DC. As a teenager, I was always intrigued by the magic of business. I remember, in particular, an early fascination with the success of McDonald's and its ability to earn profits on a 15¢ hamburger.

From my high school days as a part-time bank employee, I was encouraged to pursue the banking business by my father,

Vernon W. Hill, a residential real estate broker who had worked as a bank employee before the Second World War. When I was in high school, he was involved with a group that started a small bank in Vienna, and I worked there over a couple of summer vacations. I really liked it, and I had an aptitude for it.

Dad always wanted a son of his to attend the University of Pennsylvania's Wharton School of Business. In 1963, since I was the oldest, I made my first trip north of Washington to the Penn campus, stuck around, and graduated from Wharton with a degree in economics in 1967.

But the carefree life of the college student wasn't in the cards for me. While a full-time student at Wharton, I also worked full-time in the banking industry, first for Philadelphia National Bank and later as a commercial lender at First Peoples Bank in southern New Jersey. The joke was you could not obtain a commercial mortgage in South Jersey before 12 noon "because Vernon is still in class."

When I left Wharton, my choices were to stay where I was or go to a big bank. Irving Trust, a famous New York bank, offered me a job in its management training program. Its headquarters were based at the most glamorous business address in the world, One Wall Street. (In 2005, incidentally, we opened a Commerce Bank across the street at *Two* Wall Street.) I decided to stay in South Jersey, but I left banking and went into the real estate development business.

Following the entrepreneurial direction of my successful father, I created Site Development, a real estate development business focused on serving the needs of national retail clients. My task was to go out and find new sites, which they had to approve; then I got the site zoned for them, and they built the stores. I got paid only on success.

My first client was McDonald's Corporation, for which our company developed sites throughout America. I even had the opportunity to personally show sites to the man who built

McDonald's from a single location, Ray Kroc himself. I eventually developed 100 sites for McDonald's and another 1,000 for other companies.

(I'm still active in the retail real estate development business today. And in 1985, I partnered with Steven Lewis to acquire 25 Burger King restaurants in Pennsylvania, returning to my fast-food experience. The company now has more than 40 units in numerous states.)

Banking, however, was always my first love and in 1972, at the age of 26, I gathered a small group of investors to raise the $1.5 million needed to obtain a new New Jersey bank charter. On June 29, 1973, Commerce Bank opened for business in Marlton, New Jersey, with one office and nine team members.

When we opened that first store, we had a contest to give away an expensive red bicycle. It went on for a month, and every day one kid stuffed the ballot box—he filled out ten ballots a day. When we finally picked a winner, it was the kid. It *had* to be him. So we called and told him he had won. We were so excited for him—he really wanted that bike.

"Could I have the cash instead?" he said.

I was disappointed. We thought the kid couldn't afford a bike. I should have *recruited* him!

*

At Harvard, many years later, as we discussed the business school's Commerce Bank case study, they asked me about my marketing research before choosing Commerce Bank's predominant color scheme—red. I answered, "Shirley and I laid out the newspapers on the floor and found that no competitor used red. And so the Commerce 'Red' was born."

*

My wife and I are both Leos. You might wonder about how two lions could live under the same sign, but we both have different skill sets and the same appreciation and striving for perfection and working every day to make it better.

I remember that when Shirley first started her business, she told my father how great it was going to be and what she had done to put it all in place. He seemed somewhat excited but then he said to her, "Come and see me in five years." Dad told Shirley that there's always an excitement about starting a business and that it breeds a kind of infectious enthusiasm. "We Americans love what's new," he said. "But in year two and three and four and 23 and 30, how do you get up every morning and keep it fresh and still look to improve?"

Fortunately, Shirley and I never lost the drive to keep our businesses—and our marriage—fresh. Whether you see that as a skill set or a creed, it's the way we look at life and I think we enhance each other because of it.

*

I always believed that the world did not need another "Me, Too" bank. I believed that the value of a bank is in its deposit base. I set out to build a power retailing company modeled on the successful retailers of America rather than a typical bank.

I had been influenced by the retail phenomenon of McDonald's, and I had been a fan before I was doing development for them. By necessity, I set out to figure a better way of delivering the banking experience.

You have to understand what a bank is. A bank has two sides: a lending side and a deposit side. A bank accepts deposits and uses the money to make loans. That's been the core of banking for thousands of years. The conventional banking philosophy, then and now, is that lending is where all the value is created, that deposits are important but lending is much more important, and that the retail experience and service don't exist. The exceptions are community banks that know that deposits are their lifeblood.

I always saw a bank as a government license to borrow money cheaply. Anybody can make loans, but only licensed banks can accept deposits, so I always saw that the legal and economic value of a bank was in gathering deposits.

How were we going to compete against the whole world and gather deposits? Because I was influenced by this retailing model, I always saw the banking business as one where you focused first on gathering deposits, but you adopted the best practices of the best retailers, not the banks. Then, over time, the trick wasn't just to get more deposits, it was to get more deposits at a lower cost.

The secret of Commerce Bank—and now Metro Bank—was that not only did we have the most rapidly growing deposit base, we also had the lowest cost of deposit funding. The customer exchanged what they considered a better retail experience, of which ours was one, for a lower yield on their money—giving us more of their low-cost money. We competed on *service*—not price.

Commerce Bank was built on the theme of "America's Most Convenient Bank" and developed into one of the nation's most successful banks. In the beginning, Commerce had an original staff of nine with one office. By 2006, the bank had more than 14,000 employees with 440 offices in eight states and Washington, DC, and had redefined the banking business by delivering unsurpassed service and convenience.

In 2001, Commerce made its debut in Manhattan with two stores. The bank eventually opened in 270 locations in New York State and attracted $25 billion in deposits, making metropolitan New York the largest Commerce market.

In mid-2005, Commerce began its expansion into the Metropolitan Washington, DC, market with ten stores. In early 2006, Commerce expanded its marketplace again by opening stores in Palm Beach County, Florida.

In 2007, Commerce Bank was sold to Toronto-based TD Bank for $8.5 billion, producing a 30-year, 23 percent annual shareholder return. Everyone profited, including shareholders and team members.

As *Forbes* reported in the 20–20–20 Club in 2006, only seven companies had a CEO serving 20-plus years with a 20 percent compounded return. We were proud to come fourth on that list, behind Lawrence J. Ellison (Oracle), Howard Solomon (Forest Labs) and Warren E. Buffett (Berkshire Hathaway).

*

As I went into new markets, from Philadelphia to Manhattan to London, the established local bankers told me that their market was different from all the others we were in and that our model had to be adapted to suit them. When I stopped hiring people who believed that, our machine started to work. If you have a successful model and you believe in it, it doesn't matter what the establishment says.

Our model was just as effective in North Jersey or downtown Philly or DC or Manhattan, or even in London. We made up our minds that we wanted local people with local flavor in each market—running *our* model.

Commerce Bank hit multiple walls along the way to $50 billion in assets and $8 billion in market value. We had to evolve, our management had to evolve, the capabilities of our people had to evolve and grow. If we hadn't evolved, we would have become road kill.

And now we have found another market, London, where our unique model also adds tremendous customer and shareholder value, and where we will continue to evolve.

As you create your own unique model, you, your management and the model need to continually grow and improve. Your choices are to improve and grow or calcify and die.

Part 2

Marketing is *Everything*

3

Fans Not Customers

The greatest luxury is time, and service can help you make the most of that. Give greater productivity, greater enjoyment—what better luxury can there be?

Isadore Sharp, founder, Four Seasons Hotels and Resorts

There are customers, and there are fans. Customers are those people who come in, who bank with us, and who are almost indifferent to us. It's that convenience model, it's proximity; we are either in their building or around the corner, and they come to us. They start out being absolutely indifferent, and they are customers. We are perfectly happy having customers. But our goal is to convert them to *fans*.

Fans are customers who embrace your model and culture, become part of your community, and convert their friends to new customers of your brand.

The dimension that fans add is that willingness, when somebody is whinging about their bank or some banking tactic, to say, "Oh, go to Metro, that's *my* bank!" Or when they see one of us away from the bank wearing a red Metro "M" pin, they walk up and say, "You work for Metro Bank?" And they quickly add, "That's *my* bank. I love that bank."

Every day, people say to Metro Bank team members, "I love this bank; I just *love* this bank. Every day, you do something that I never expected you to do. When I go into your stores, employees say 'Hello,' 'Thank you,' they call me by my name, they tell me to have a great day, 'Is there anything else I can do for you?' I don't feel like there are any gimmicks or games being played when I come in to do banking."

When people talk about a bank that way, it's because we have created fans as opposed to customers.

If you don't do business with Metro Bank, you'll probably read this and think, "Come on! It's a bank, for crying out loud." The objective part of you cries out, "Banking is a commodity. One is just like the next and the next." (*And Apple is just a computer company!*) But there are people who sing our praises in centers of influence, to their neighbors, to someone they don't know sitting on the bus or tube seat next to them—and therein lies the *fan*.

Fifty percent of a company's business comes from family and friends saying, "I love that company." And to us therein lies the difference between screaming, raving fans and mere customers. Customers are indifferent. They like us, but they might never give us a rousing endorsement in a public place. That's the difference. And the more fans you have, it's like dispatching evangelists or disciples to sell your product.

The result of building fans was the internal deposit growth at Commerce Bank of 25 percent a year, compounded over 30 years.

Every great business will build fans.

*

How do we create fans?

A man came into a Metro Bank store one evening and left his cheque book on his customer service representative's desk. After he left, the CSR saw it, got his name and account, checked his identification and gave him a ring on his mobile. It was after 8pm and the store was essentially closed. The customer was relieved to know his financial information was secure and figured he'd come in the next day to collect it. But our CSR said, "Tell me where you are." It was 8.30pm and he was at a pub about ten minutes away with friends. The CSR said, "I walk past there on my way home. I'll pop in and drop it off." He went into the pub and found the customer sitting around a table with ten friends. The CSR walked over and returned the cheque book. Not long after, the CSR received an email saying, "Thank you! All my friends were blown away and they're all going to come and open accounts because that was just so amazing."

Nobody said to the CSR, "Do that." It's not something that will ever be found in an employee manual. That's just somebody doing the right thing. And that simple kindness created a fan within that person and ten more potential fans because their friend blurted out, "Wasn't that amazing?"

If other banks have fans, I haven't heard a lot about them. When I talk to the few friends I have who don't bank with us, for reasons like location or rate, I won't succumb to giving them a better rate just to earn their business. I am happy to listen to them whinge and remind them that the extra quarter of a percent they get is really worth all their aggravation.

Ultimately, we do things because our customers will love it, because it will help us create fans. That attitude is lost on traditional career bankers. I don't think that they do have raving fans. Spending time among them at industry events, I get the sense that they themselves are not convinced that they deserve fans.

*

Emotional brands create massive value; building fans not customers creates emotional brands.

There are different kinds of brands. There's the basic brand where the name relates to a product. There are other brands where you feel good about them. But there are legendary brands where the experience overwhelms the product and those brands create fans. And, of course, Apple continues to be the best example of this.

The fast-food model influenced much of what we do at Metro Bank, from making all channels accessible to consumers to saturating communities with stores for their convenience and treating every customer, large or small, like royalty.

The Home Depot, under its co-founders, Bernie Marcus and Arthur Blank, was a company that inspired a legion of loyal, devoted fans. Men gave up their neighborhood hardware stores in droves to go to a place that excelled at carrying every product that they could possibly imagine they needed and more they never even dreamed of but with which they still fell in love.

We want evangelists for our brand. We want brand ambassadors who spread the word about us, people who are passionate about us as a company because we've exceeded their expectations at every contact and opportunity. Every person we recruit, every person who works for our companies, passionately believes in not just doing an okay job, but doing the best possible job they can and creating the best customer experience they can.

I believe that all customers have value; most bankers will tell you that only their biggest depositors and borrowers are important. Metro Bank treats everyone equally well. ˙

Our job and our responsibility are to make an emotional connection with our customers first, but then to go above and beyond, exceeding their expectations when it comes to customer service, so they become fans. Customers will show up and dutifully do business with us. But *fans* will tell their friends and neighbors about Metro Bank, helping us grow our company because of their personal satisfaction.

We have never fired anybody for giving too much service. That will never happen.

In London, where customer service expectations in banks are so low, one of our CSRs started talking to a man about his background and where he grew up. Small talk, but he was so impressed by her genuine interest that he burst into tears of happiness in the store. He said that no one working in a bank had ever wanted to know that much about him.

Sometimes, in addition to simply helping a customer open a new account, we might give them a tour of the store. In so doing, we can explain why we do things the way we do, demonstrating in words and deeds what services will be available to them.

We'll walk them over to the Magic Money Machine and point out that it will count their coins for free and provide a voucher that can be exchanged for cash. The Magic Money Machines are for adults and children alike. You'll find one in each of our stores ready to count your saved coins. They're free to use and great fun if you want to guess the value of your coins with our interactive game—you could even win a prize.

Our machines sort the coins for you so you don't need to, and there's no limit to the value of coins you can bring in—a great excuse to save more.

When a customer uses the Magic Money Machine for the first time, it usually goes something like this:

The customer dumps a jar of coins in, gets a receipt, and hands it to a cashier.

"Would you like me to put this in your account, or would you like it back in notes?" the cashier asks.

"Just take out what I owe you for the cost of doing this and put the rest in my account."

"There is no cost for doing this. This is absolutely free."

"*Free*? Why is it free?"

"Because it's part of our service," the cashier will say. "It's part of what our organization is about."

And when a non-customer uses the coin-counting machine for the first time, we do the same thing:

"Would you like us to put the money in your account, or would you like it back in notes?"

"Well, I am not a customer."

"Well, why don't you become a customer?" the cashier will say.

It becomes an instant opportunity to persuade that person to become a customer of the bank, and we will hopefully get them to open an account on the spot. If not, they leave with the impression, "I don't even bank here, and they did this for me, and it didn't cost me anything." And eventually, we will get that customer back.

When we first started building Metro Bank, there was a lot of skepticism about us. People just weren't sure. But we never gave up, we just kept calling on them, calling on them, and calling on them again. The customer would eventually say, "I hear more from you than I do from my current bank," and the other bank would eventually do something stupid that would provide us with an opportunity to get that business. And when we had the opportunity to get it, we didn't make any mistakes, and we got it.

We might get a letter from a housewife that says, "I can't believe how great your people treated me. I was in the branch with three kids, they were screaming and yelling. I had a problem with my current account and your people gave the kids coloring books, lollipops and settled them down, and we were able to fix my problem."

CEOs send us letters saying, "I just want to tell you how much I appreciate the relationship we have and the time that you have taken to talk about my business, understand my business, and get into the nuts and bolts of what makes my business go. I feel confident that our relationship is strong and will continue to prosper now and in the future."

In New York, not only did we not have a clue how wildly successful we would be, but we didn't know how popular the coin counters would be. In 2006 alone, they were used 6 million times. Some days we found bullets banging around in them. There were foreign coins, washers and, on one occasion, we had canine items that belonged in pooper-scoopers.

Sometimes, inevitably, a store's machine is down for maintenance and someone gets disappointed. Once, in Manhattan, a customer came in dragging a huge water jug filled with coins. Our employees called the closest store to the location where the machine was out of service, made sure that their machine was up, and put the customer in a cab. Then our people met the cab at the corner of the other store, paid the fare, took the jug and counted the coins.

Those examples speak to the human spirit of our staffers. Here are some new ones from Metro Bank stores:

- An elderly woman said she hated doing business with plastic cards and much preferred cheques. We told her that we printed both in our stores. That weekend, she transferred her accounts—totaling £250,000—from her previous bank to ours all because she kept running out of cheques and they couldn't keep pace.

- A customer lost his wallet out of town and was stuck. He rang us up and said, "I really have a problem here. I've lost my wallet. I can't get a ticket. I can't get home. What can you do?" We checked his account and he had plenty of money in it. We rang the ticket office in Reading where he was sitting. We paid for his ticket over the phone. That was all done by somebody at the call center. We knew nothing about it until he came in the next day and told a manager that the experience was "Genuinely amazing!"

At other British financial institutions, just to put these events in perspective, most employees wouldn't have even thought of taking any of these extra steps. They have processes to follow and the processes are considered more important than actually thinking. It wouldn't have entered their minds, whereas we encourage our team members to act independently and in the moment. We give them the stories and tell them this is what we empower them to do. Anywhere else, the team member at the call center would have probably been told off for taking too long on her calls—it took 40 minutes to get the stranded customer a ticket and get him to the right booth to collect it. *We* made a big fuss about it: we made that team member a star.

Here is another example.

When we discover somebody opening a new account on their birthday we'll often round up several CSRs and sing an impromptu "Happy Birthday" just to make them feel special.

It's instilling these behaviors in our team members that really makes the difference between Metro Bank and the "Me, Too" bank across the street. I'm a firm believer that anybody can copy your products. Anybody can copy your hours, your colors and your money handling policies, but they cannot copy your culture because that is the very fabric of who you are and why you are different. We are defined by the way we answer customer questions, the way we give them accurate and timely information, and the way we make sure that they leave very, very happy.

Our never-ending goal is to surprise and delight.

*

One of the unique characteristics of Metro Bank—and formerly of Commerce Bank—is that everybody works together. There are no silos and no agendas. We stand shoulder to shoulder, aligned for the good of the customer, for the good of the bank. That is our mindset, pure and simple.

We grew Commerce Bank's commercial business every year. There were many reasons for that. We went out and saw our customers face-to-face. We went to their places of business. We wanted to know who they were, where they've been, where they are, and where they want to go. We strove to understand their business goals and plans. And just as important, we wanted them to understand us. This was pure relationship banking. We never did deals for the sake of doing the deal, no matter how good the loan might have been.

When an account officer goes to a customer's workplace with their Metro Bank boss—or sometimes even with the bank president or CEO—it builds the relationship like nothing else. Customers love it when we visit them at their place of business. They love it when senior management takes an interest.

When Metro Bank officers have a big loan that needs senior approval from headquarters, they tell their customer that it has to be reviewed by Craig or Vernon. Their reaction isn't, "Who are those guys?" because they probably already know at least one of us. Customers in every market have a chance to meet our senior executives and develop a personal relationship. Where else in Britain except Metro Bank can the customers meet the founder or the CEO? Nobody here has ever seen a bank CEO in a branch before.

These relationships reinforce the unparalleled quality of our loan portfolio. They put us in a position to react quickly to our customers' credit needs. They put us in a position where, if a customer is having a hiccup with their business, they don't run and hide from us. They come in and talk to us, and they say, "Look, I've got a little problem. Here's what I need. Here's what I can do for you in the meantime in the way of more collateral or more guarantee," and we can and will work through the problem.

The other benefit of our relationships is that these same customers love referring their own clients and suppliers to us. We build the bulk of our business in that way. It is *real* relationship banking.

4

Putting the "Grand" in Grand Openings

If I had a brick for every time I've repeated the phrase Quality, Service, Cleanliness and Value, I think I'd probably be able to bridge the Atlantic Ocean with them.

Ray Kroc, founder, McDonald's

For months, as we constructed the first Metro Bank, the average Londoner passing our location couldn't begin to guess what was going on behind the 15-foot tall windows facing out onto the street. They were teased with a simple, unfamiliar and unlikely sentiment: "Love Your Bank At Last."

At a time when no British high street banking establishment enjoyed an inspiring customer satisfaction rating—and, in fact, most were under 20 percent—the idea that anyone in the UK could love a bank seemed absurd.

More than 100,000 people a day went past those windows, thanks to their proximity to Holborn tube station. It was a joke to some, a mystery to others. Newspapers and TV news reports picked up on the signs and did frequent updates on our progress, talking about these "crazy people" who want to start a new bank.

Needless to say, we were discouraged from hosting live

bands, stilt walkers and free food. But we stuck to our guns and proceeded with the first Metro Bank grand opening circus.

The Americans in our operation were cautious about misinterpreting and underestimating the cultural differences between the Yanks and the Brits. We were getting good advance press, but what if nobody showed up?

Two days before we opened, that fear was allayed. A producer from the BBC One "Breakfast" show called and asked, "Can we broadcast our morning show live from Holborn during your grand opening?" (This was the equivalent of NBC's "Today" show making a similar request in the US. It was that big a deal.)

We said, "Yes," of course, and amid all our other preparations, added a layer of staff to work with the TV crew's 4am arrival to prepare for a 6–9am live telecast from inside the first Metro Bank store.

The night before, we decided not to take any chances on opening and nobody showing up. We asked our property agent to come in that morning and officially open an account on camera and asked the entire opening day staff to give similar invitations to friends and family. "We've got to have people at the front door, queuing up, at 8am. What if we're on the BBC and nobody shows up?"

It was a fail-safe move, and in retrospect it seems silly to have wasted energy worrying about it. But our trepidation the night before was palpable.

What did happen that morning was that BBC One was simply the TV network that phoned ahead for permission to broadcast from our site; in total, media from 36 different countries showed up, sending reporters to interview, shoot video, record audio and take photographs. There were British, European, Australian, American, Japanese and even North Korean TV production trucks lining the streets, all sent to do a story on a bank opening in London! That's how bad the existing British banking industry's reputation had become.

Customers poured in but they barely outnumbered the reporters and camera operators. Thank goodness the live BBC One broadcast encouraged more people to come out and experience Metro Bank in person.

Meanwhile, we opened accounts on the spot, instantly issuing debit cards and credit cards—something unheard of in London, where customers typically apply to a bank and wait a couple of weeks to actually join their exclusive club and get their card and pin. There were bands playing outside, where Shirley and I greeted prospective customers alongside our Yorkshire terrier Duffy, who welcomed their dogs, as well as colorful stilt walkers and beaming team members who distributed free food (including 8,000 bags of popcorn) and drinks, balloons, shoe shines and manicures.

"We were overwhelmed by the customer response," CEO Craig Donaldson said later.

The Holborn store has a grand staircase and, from its top, we looked out on the street and witnessed waves of humanity. You'd think The Beatles had reunited and were expected to arrive at any moment!

It was glorious mayhem. And that was just the *first* day. The grand opening continued for three days, but the atmosphere of excitement and magic continues to this day.

*

We recruited former Commerce Bank team members as job captains for the opening. They supervised the initial operation and guided new hires through a tumultuous start. We left nothing to chance.

After they opened a new account, we directed them to an area where they could choose a "Welcome!" gift. That was a new and amazing experience for many, but nothing could beat being able to open an account in minutes and walk out with a new

debit card and a PIN that they had chosen. A first in the UK—
just like in the US.

*

On the night of the grand opening we had planned a dinner at
the Gherkin (the former site of the Baltic Exchange, at 30 St Mary
Axe, which acquired its unofficial name because the building is
pickle-shaped) as a celebration for investors, board members
and some Metro Bank executives. As it turned out, no executives
made it because they were still serving new customers.

*

Every new Metro Bank store celebrates its opening in similarly
grand style for two full days, Friday and Saturday.

We blitz the area for two weeks before, handing out cards
that offer the bearer £20 to switch their account to Metro Bank.
We also tell them to bring the family and even the dog—everybody is welcome at the party.

The excitement starts in earnest on the previous Wednesday
with a VIP party for neighboring businesses and politicians in
selected locations. Thursday is for stocking the store with food
and new customer gifts, followed by the grand opening hoopla
on Friday and Saturday. We're open seven days a week, so that
first weekend is rounded out by a soft Sunday to get ready for the
first full week of business and to welcome pleasantly surprised
customers who aren't expecting to find a neighborhood bank
open on the seventh day.

The big openings started in the earliest days of Commerce
Bank because we were going into new locations all the time
where people didn't know us. It's a great way to make a splash.
The event announces to the local community, "This isn't what
you'd normally expect of a bank!" It speaks to our policy of

The Media Reacts to the Grand Opening of Metro Bank UK

"Metro Bank is a force for banking good … Metro Bank is something to sing about."

Jeff Prestridge, *Daily Mail*, March 18, 2011

"As far as *This Is Money* knows, walking out at Holborn station on a Thursday morning doesn't usually involve dodging blue and red clad women wobbling around on stilts, shoe shiners, a live jazz band or feeding biscuits to excitable dogs."

Tara Evans, *This Is Money*, August 2, 2010

"Upstart shakes up banking sector with full service on Sunday."

Phillip Inman, *Guardian*, August 1, 2010

"Shoppers piling out of Holborn tube station on their way to Covent Garden today will be greeted by an unusual sight: a bank open for business on a Sunday."

Jill Treanor, *Observer*, August 1, 2010

"Amidst the razzmatazz of balloons and a trad jazz band playing outside, I found real interest from the first customers, not just idle curiosity."

Ian Pollock, BBC News, July 29, 2010

"Metro Bank will focus on Greater London for its first ten years. Now that it has opened it raises a rather obvious question…Why hasn't anyone thought of doing this before?"

Ian Pollock, BBC News, July 29, 2010

"Metro Bank opens on Sunday as battle for high street hots up."

Jill Treanor, *Observer*, August 1, 2010

"Ready to do business: first high street bank in 100 years opens its doors (and will only shut them four days a year)."

Sean Poulter, *Daily Mail*, July 30, 2010

"This was no ordinary Thursday morning. It was the grand opening of the UK's first start up bank in over 100 years, Metro Bank, and they sure had put on a show."

Tara Evans, *This Is Money*, August 2, 2010

"Metro Bank looks like it could be up to the task, putting excellent customer service at the top of its agenda."

Jane Baker, Lovemoney.com, July 29, 2010

"Hundreds of customers flocked to Holborn yesterday after the first high street bank to launch in Britain for more than 100 years opened its doors."

Jamie Dunkley, *Daily Telegraph*, July 29, 2010

"Metro Bank has promised to revolutionise the British banking experience by offering retail opening hours, unparalleled service and a range of products it pledges are suitable for everyone."

Jamie Dunkley, *Daily Telegraph*, July 29, 2010

"exceed expectations" and "surprise and delight" in every way possible.

Why do we make grand openings such a production? That's easy: first impressions are lasting. The elements that create a spectacular launch are basically what the brand offers and how well it is executed. Our grand openings are almost like putting together a Broadway or West End show. Everyone has a role, from store captains and section leaders to runners. When the doors open to the public, everyone is well rehearsed and knows exactly what they are to do; no one deviates from that. Execution is everything.

For example, we don't want customer service representatives—whose primary job during a new store opening is to set up new accounts—to waste time because something they need isn't at hand. We have what we call "runners", whose sole task is to be close by to get whatever the CSR needs to stay fully involved with the prospective new customer. When a deposit has to be made and a premium gift provided, we have prearranged signals for runners to come to the desk and pick up a deposit and return moments later with a welcome gift.

Team leaders wear headsets and are assigned sections of the store to monitor. If there is a question or an issue, or an approval is needed, that's a "bump it up". The bump it up person will come over and do their best to say "Yes" to whatever the customer needs.

The back room is crucial during a grand opening to make sure that deposits are processed appropriately and quickly; that all the necessary paperwork gets done correctly; that proper identification is taken; and that the gift is handed out and tracked.

It's complicated. We hold grand opening training sessions so there are few surprises for even the greenest of team members and they know exactly what to do and how to do it. It's really something to see. Team members from already open stores always help staff these sunup-to-sundown events, providing experience—and relief—to new associates. (And it doesn't hurt ambitious team members to see and be seen by the bank's leadership.)

There are greeters at the door to welcome everyone who

comes in and a waiting-list host or hostess who manages the flow so that no one queues unnecessarily. If there is a wait of any kind, we will give the customer a coupon to get a cup of coffee nearby at Eat or Pret a Manger, and we'll hand out a beeper that will signal it's time to return and open an account.

The grand opening is extremely important to our brand because we're welcoming the community to come into our store and bank with us. We want their experience to be different and better than anywhere else that they have ever been.

Often we'll hire performing dogs, which are guaranteed to draw a crowd. We have people outside the store who we call "blitzers"; they hand out red Metro Bank balloons to children, put Metro Bank bandanas on dogs, and generally engage people to come on in and see what we're about.

Every great company includes a "fun" element in its model that engages and enthralls its customers with never-ending surprise and delight.

Celebrate your openings, celebrate your new customers. And celebrate that you are becoming part of a new community. If you make it an event, if you *believe* it is an event, your customers will, too.

5
The New Math

I am not making watches only to look at the time. I am making jewels! They are jewels!

Nicolas Hayek, founder, Swatch

Every decision you make will strengthen or weaken your brand. In the long term, a reinforcing client base is more important than how much you make in the next quarter.

We have developed a number of formulas to explain the way we do things, including:

$$Model + Culture + Execution = Fans$$

The Metro Bank model demands that we always exceed our customers' expectations by providing superior products, services, facilities, and delivery channels. Metro Bank is a power retailer determined to do all of this.

Distinctively designed stores, unbeatable hours, legendary personalized service, cutting-edge technology, and no-fee policies enable Metro Bank to attract customers to a unique banking experience and grow deposits at exceptional, predictable rates.

The value of a bank is its low-cost core deposit base. Deposit gathering is banking's unique advantage. Anyone can make loans. Only banks can accept deposits.

The elements of the differentiated Metro Bank model are:

- deposit focus;
- customer value added;
- a great retail experience, always;
- the best facilities in the best location;
- no stupid bank rules;
- revenue growth driven, not cost driven.

Our brand is who we are. It is what our customers expect. And it is our most valuable asset. Our primary responsibility is thus threefold:

- **Protect the brand**—*do nothing stupid*!
- **Refine the brand**—*make it better all the time*!
- **Expand the brand**—*find new products and new areas where we can add value*!

Metro Bank's culture is our social fabric, our DNA. It matches our model and is pervasive throughout the organization. It allows us to share and execute a common mission.

The thing about culture is that you can't merge it, you can't acquire it, and you can't convert it. Our culture is the spirit that enables our company to excel. A melding of a unique model and a reinforcing culture is unique to Metro Bank.

It's not as if we woke up and said, "Okay, here's a new strategy for tomorrow," or "Here's what we'll do next week, which is different from what we did last week." We have been doing business our way forever. It's our heritage. It's our personality. It's who we are.

We do the right things for the right reasons. We put the customer first at all costs and profit from the adventure that brings.

We seek people that we believe will embrace the culture,

"street" bankers who hustle for business every day. Those are the people whose own culture and personality match us best.

The words "I can't" aren't in our team's vocabulary. When I ask something of them, such as "Get the new store open in four days," the response is more pointed: "I'll *find* a way to do it."

The concept of creating superior products and services is just the foundation. At Metro Bank, we understand that improving the customer experience and building a base of professionals who believe in the company's mission has been key to our success. Metro Bank attracts people with energy, ambition and a passion for providing AMAZE!ing service to our customers.

Sometimes compared to a theme park atmosphere, the corporate culture at Metro Bank is truly unique. From Metro-red balloons and attire to our Mr. "M" logo mascot, the culture shared by Metro Bank team members is one of excitement and passion about taking superior customer service to new heights.

We want our customers to be passionate about doing business with Metro Bank, to become Metro fans. We call our intense dedication to exceeding customers' expectations our "AMAZE! the Customer" philosophy. Metro Bank University, our employee training center, immerses our team members in the AMAZE! the Customer culture from the very beginning. It doesn't take new hires long to see that our philosophy is much more than just a corporate mission statement: it's a way of life.

Our corporate spirit—something we've made a unique part of our social fabric—enables us to succeed. A company can have a great model with a reinforcing culture, but execution determines its fate. Great retailers know that it's what happens at the store level—at the point of customer contact—not at the corporate level, which determines the fate of a company. Retail is *detail*.

We are fanatically focused on delivering a unique customer experience. Over-investment in facilities, training and people, a focused geographic management, and countless mystery shops a year ensure that we always exceed our customers' expectations.

These are the keys to fanatical execution:

- Believe in your model.
- Over-invest in facilities and people.
- Demand 100 percent execution.

Great retailers know that the execution of a great model determines a company's success. Our market management system delivers a unique customer experience at every point of contact, backed by the technological and financial strength of a growing regional financial services company. The strength of our model enables us to over-invest in people, training and facilities.

Retail + Entertainment = Metro Bank

As I study the history of retailing, two things stand out. One is that no great retailer was ever created by making acquisitions. All the great ones did it by wandering around, figuring out a model that could survive, refining it, and then expanding it.

In the retail business, you don't have to be 100 percent better than the competition in order to beat them. You have to be 15 percent better, and you have to get better all the time. Another secret of Metro Bank is that we are never happy with what we have; we know we have to get better.

Second, I believe that there are few or no examples of seriously broken big retail models that have ever been fixed. When you get past the point that your people, procedures, facilities, and delivery are broken, the customers have a clear perception that your model is broken, and that's impossible to fix.

There are a lot of banks in the world. Too many, probably, but it's no different from the explosion of corner shops at every well-trafficked intersection, or even the number of books this one competed with for your attention in a real or virtual bookstore.

It's all about standing out from the competition, creating

visual appeal both in the store and for passersby on foot and in cars or buses.

Great retailers create fun experiences for their customers, turning them into fans. Just because we are in the banking business doesn't mean the experience has to be dull. Our ATMs are fun and appeal to children and adults alike. You can bring your dog into any Metro Bank store and it will find a biscuit, a water dish and a Metro Bank scarf waiting. There are bright red lollipops for the kids. The lighting is brilliant and exciting. And you can experience all this any day of the week, because every Metro Bank store is open seven days a week from early morning until late at night. We are there for our customers' convenience; we don't make them bend their schedules to our whims.

Probably the best example of how we do this is by providing in-store service seven days a week, every week.

We opened in 1973 with Saturday hours and long hours the very first day. Not as long as we have now, but longer than was common. We were open daily from 8am to 8pm and on Saturdays from 9am to noon. Saturday hours were revolutionary then.

During that time, Old Guard banks would open on Saturdays, then think better of it. But then we went to *Sunday* hours at every location, which was a tipping point in this company. We didn't think people would want to bank with us that much on Sunday—although, in fact, they do—but it sent a message to customers that we are there for their convenience, not for ours.

Our original long hours were meant to send the same message. But Sunday put us over the top.

To this day, Old Guard bankers tell me I am nuts. "You shouldn't be open on Sunday, you can't be open on Sunday," they say. Then they ask, "How do you hire people to work on Sunday?"

That's the dumbest question I ever hear out of the mouths of Old Guard bankers. "Let's see," I say. "Every mall is open on Sunday, every retailer is open on Sunday, but banks can't find staff on Sundays?"

Bankers believe that there is some mystique about bank employees or some mystique about running a branch bank. Believe me, this is Retailing 101. There is only one type of customer. It is easy to say, what does any customer want? They want service, they want the convenience, they want to come in and be treated like our best customer.

For example, we open ten minutes before the announced time and close ten minutes later. We think like a customer and always exceed their expectations.

Great Ideas + Excellent Execution = The Never-ending Story

Here's what happens in most large companies. There are all these different areas reporting to chief officers including compliance, marketing, operations, audits, and all of them have a point of view that reflects their area. Somebody must filter all that out and say, "What do their individual concerns do to our brand?" When the company doesn't have a keeper of the brand—whether that person is the founder or a subsequent protector and evangelist—performance and perception weaken.

There is a NatWest bank branch next door to our store in Uxbridge, west London. During the first day of our two-day grand opening celebration, NatWest put out a signboard in front of their store that said, "NatWest customers, we are thinking about extending our hours." It didn't say that they would do it—or when!

Another NatWest office *did* open on a Saturday to compete with us, but they would not allow banking transactions. So why were they open? It beats us.

One of the other high street banks extended its hours during the 2012 Olympics, but once the Olympics ended, so were the extended hours.

Another anti-customer behavior we observed was that *many London banks put an end to the practice of offering safe deposit boxes.* Considering the nonsensical way most British banks offered the service in the first place, this might not have been a bad idea.

In the US, almost every bank offers secure safe deposit box services. Boxes come in standardized sizes—small, medium and large—provided by the bank. Usually two keys are required to unlock them: one kept by the customer, the other by the bank. And they are stored in a vault that is sealed when the bank is not open.

In the UK, we observed a very different approach. If you want a safe deposit box, you have to buy your own at a hardware store. It could be metal, plastic or even cardboard. It could lock—or not. And where does the bank store it? Heaven knows.

My wife and I opened a safe deposit box at the Barclays branch down the street from the Metro Bank in Hounslow, west London. We wanted to test the British system and went to the bank to retrieve something from our box.

First, good luck getting help from a customer "service" rep. Our request was met with eye rolls and sighs as we were handed from one unhelpful employee to another. And we still have no idea where our box was stored because they wouldn't tell or show us.

While many British banks were writing off this service, we recognized it as an enormous business opportunity. The Asian community is especially enamored of safe deposit boxes in the UK and the US. (In New York at Commerce Bank and in London at Metro Bank, we installed thousands of boxes in stores in neighborhoods with large Asian populations.)

British bank employees don't appear to trust each other, so management can't send just one person to retrieve a box. And because there are all those different sizes and types of boxes, it takes these bank employees forever to find the right one. We've also heard multiple reports of lost boxes.

When you finally complete your business and return the box, the bank employees roll their eyes again and sometimes shove your box of valuables on the floor underneath the counter until someone can be bothered to put it away "properly."

And just in case our experience was unique, we sent Metro Bank employees to five more high street banks with similar results.

At Metro Bank stores, we provide standardized, numbered, double-locked safe deposit boxes. Our customers can see exactly where we keep their valuables and they are welcome to come in at any time.

*

There are four myths of UK retail banking:

- The first is that *no one switches bank accounts*. It must be true because I read it in a London newspaper: people in the UK get divorced more frequently than they switch their accounts. *But it's not true!* Certainly not since July 2010. We're opening up so many new accounts, it's crazy. We surpassed the creation of 100,000 new accounts far sooner than we ever dreamed possible.

- The second is that *rate is everything*. People will come in for great service. They are willing to give up some rate for extraordinary service. Our deposit rates are competitive, but our service is our competitive advantage.

- The third is that *a bank can only make money by cutting costs*. Of course not! There are two ways to make money. Grow your top line—that's the best way. Cost cutting, in my mind, is the road to extinction.

- The fourth, of course, is that *the branch is dead*. No way, no how. Not by the volume of in-store traffic that we see. We continually prove that retail customers want the best in every delivery channel and they want the freedom to choose those channels every day. **Our stores are lifelines to our customers.**

When we first opened in Holborn, we had employees of other banks walking in and asking to join us because we threw such a great opening party. Barclays tried to do something to peel off our foot traffic and it was hilarious watching them retaliate. Every day they did something different—and increasingly desperate. First they handed out balloons. The next day they dressed the staff in old-fashioned garb to show how old they were, how old the bank was. I'm sure that enticed people, right? The next day they dressed the same folk up in a more seductive way and had them pole dancing against streetlights. It was crazy! We just watched and laughed. By the end of that week, many of their embarrassed employees crossed the street and inquired about jobs with us.

*

Customers in New York City were an interesting group. As soon as our retail brand came out, the consumer market responded in a typically New York way: "Now *that's* what I'm talking about! They are open when I need them. They don't charge me fees. They are not rude to me when I walk in. I don't feel like I am crossing into a demilitarized zone. Their physical locations actually look and feel great. Why aren't all banks like this?"

Great models make retailing different, rewarding and fun.

We learned over the years to take nothing for granted. Not the value of a great location and not the value of customers large and small. And we learned it's not just about the *parts* of a model; it's how they fit *together*.

Any successful model needs to be different and create customer value. As Commerce Bank expanded in New York, we had the opportunity to redefine retail banking—and we do again with Metro Bank in Greater London.

6

Love Your Bank At Last!

We only do things that are exciting to us. If it's boring, we walk away.

Daniel Lamarre, president, Cirque du Soleil

Our motto "Love Your Bank At Last" may be a little in your face, but the customer service dissatisfaction scores for banks in London are astronomically high and the number of complaints that our competition gets on a daily basis is ridiculous.

"Love Your Bank At Last" is a totally new experience in Britain and it gets to the root of our customer-centric concept.

Consumers value service and convenience. They value walking into a pleasant environment where the doors are open seven days a week. They want multiple channels and multiple access points when dealing with a business partner or a supplier of services, meaning they want it online (www.metrobankonline.co.uk), but they also want to be able to talk to somebody live. They want to be able to walk in and see somebody eyeball to eyeball.

Appearance matters, service matters, and convenience matters.

You can never be too fanatical about service. We have a goal of 100 percent customer service every time, every day, always. While that is physically impossible, it's what we really must strive for, and anything short of that is unacceptable. Once you start setting ratios of 98 percent satisfaction, it's a slippery slope to 96 percent, which is just not acceptable. You can never be too detail oriented. And it is everybody's job to care about everything. Shirley and I always shop our stores. You have to treat the business like you own it.

Metro Bank is the new and improved version of our American model. Think about it: where else will customers find a bank with extended hours that is open seven days a week? Or where the cashiers don't go to lunch during the customers' lunch hour—which is when they're going to their bank? We encountered the odd London practice of branch training on Wednesdays, where they close for unannounced lengths of time to train employees about their products. Good for them, but customers don't reliably know when their bank will be open and busy people don't have time to waste waiting around. It will open whenever the bankers finish their training, which might be 10am, or, if training takes a little bit longer, 10.15, *or later*. It's an insane, insensitive customer policy. It's all about the bankers and what is convenient for them.

A basic flaw in the British banking tradition is that institutions believe that potential customers must *apply* for an account, which is essentially applying to the *bank*. In fact, you have to make an appointment to open a new account.

In our world, to our way of thinking as a depositor, you're lending us your money. What on earth are you applying for? A private club? We should be applying and appealing to *you*.

Let me share with you the story of a pair of young British men who started their own London-based IT business. They had been under "consideration" for an account at one of the traditional high street banks. A decision was ridiculously long in the making. On a whim and out of frustration, they walked into

Metro Bank carrying a stack of customer cheques. They could not open an account anywhere else to cash these months-old cheques! We opened their account within an hour and they were thrilled to the point where they said, "If you need us for ads, if you need us for testimonials, if you need us for anything, please ask!" New fans were born.

*

"Love Your Bank at Last" is about having a mission and looking at everything through the eyes of the customer.

We didn't invent banking. What we did was fashion a model that bathes the customer in convenience, with all the services that everyone else has at fair rates and the traditional American banking idea of loving the customer and making everything work for them. The reason people hate the traditional British banks is because they don't have another option.

We tell prospective customers, "Come with us and let's see what a difference we can make in the way you're treated." Where they are accustomed to an unsexy commoditized banking and finance tradition, we present a sexy retail model.

The existing oligarchy used its monopoly power to under-invest in facilities, infrastructure, people, and service. It is saddled with legacy systems, legacy delivery channels, funding problems, capital shortages, and customer disaffection.

We begin with a clean, modern slate designed to create *FANS*.

*

If customers are going to love your business, your marketing of it must AMAZE them. The *model* is marketing. The *brand* is marketing. *Everything we do* is marketing. I say to new hires, "Everything you do, every day, makes the brand weaker or stronger."

Marketing has the widest possible meaning at Metro Bank, from the red "M" lapel pins to the red "M" cufflinks, from the red "M" door handles to the ads and everything else we can think of.

At the core of what we do is creating *FANS not customers*. We cannot maintain our growth rate unless our customers are out selling for us all the time, so everything we do reinforces the idea of fans. We are on a mission to redefine our market segment.

There are a number of general precepts under which Metro Bank operates that will translate to almost any smart business. These include:

- the establishment of emotional branding;
- brand marketing;
- decentralized delivery, centralized control;
- over-investment in real estate and fittings;
- provision of a service value proposition vis-à-vis the competition;
- uniform store design.

*

One of the greatest points of differentiation between Metro Bank and its competitors—as it was in the US with Commerce Bank—is the emphasis we put on having the best call center in the business. Not in our business but in *any* business.

The people who bank with us never see the Metro Bank customer call center, but it probably influences their opinion of us as much as anything else.

We had the number one rated call center at Commerce Bank because we had human beings answering every phone call, *24 hours a day, 7 days a week, 365 days a year*—real people answering the questions and solving the problems of real customers. It became another way to deliver our model instead of just a pain-in-the-butt call center.

And at Metro Bank, we've made delivering customer service better than everyone else in every channel in which customers want access among the highest priorities of our business.

Unlike every other call center, where you have to punch a series of buttons and endure a series of prompts, customers calling Metro Bank get a human being right away who is empowered to take care of them, whatever it takes, around the clock and around the calendar.

Who needs a "Me, Too" call center? Shouldn't we make it another great experience? At Metro Bank, it is.

*

Metro Bank is the ultimate realization of everything I learned at Commerce, reintroduced, and its success in a completely new environment reinforces the concept.

Give the customer legendary service, and one day your company will be a legend, too.

Make your customers happy and they'll become better promoters of your brand, product, and service than the best placed advertisement. Their satisfaction will boost your bottom line like nothing else.

Metro Bank is committed to growth and ours is a growth model. To grow, we must constantly reinvest in people, in processes, in systems, in training, and in facilities. Senior people at the bank are constantly thinking about how to make it better, how to improve it, how to give our customers better service, which makes it a better environment for team members as well.

7

Surprise and Delight!

Simplicity is the ultimate sophistication.

Steve Jobs, co-founder, Apple

We ask our team members to treat our business as if they own it and you should ask the same from your employees.

We want them to think. If something doesn't seem right to them, we want them to raise their hand and say, "This doesn't make sense." Or, in answer to an unusual customer request, to say, "You know what? I'm not supposed to do this, but it seems to make sense to me, so let me talk to my supervisor about why I think this should be done." Taking the extra step because it makes sense to do it, even if on an exceptional basis, is okay.

We even have a policy for that: *one to say yes, two to say no.*

In responding to customer requests, our team members have two choices: (1) say "Yes!" and solve the issue on the spot; or (2) find someone else who can.

Mistakes do happen. That's why we like to acknowledge our errors and demonstrate our ability to recover from them. If we make a mistake, recovering the right way and swiftly will gain that customer's future loyalty. We're a bank that is unafraid of apologizing and we'll even put our money where our apology is: "Here is a £20 satisfaction guarantee cheque."

To say "Yes" requires a combination of both attitude and substance—what we do and how we do it. The substance that backs up our attitude comes in four parts:

- **Product knowledge.** Know the products and services.

- **Company knowledge.** Know how the organization works so if you can't help, you know who can.

- **Listening skills.** Listen, understand, and *then* respond to the customer.

- **Problem solving skills.** Know how to fix things, and fix them fast.

Policies and procedures are designed to provide guidelines for operating our business efficiently. Sometimes they get in the way of providing excellent customer service. Whenever a customer's need conflicts, we tell our team members to use their good judgment and/or "bump it up" to a supervisor.

Other than "No," some words in combination create immediate negative images. We want to avoid these forbidden phrases, which can drive customers up the wall in anger or frustration.

Here they are with suggested alternatives:

Forbidden phrase	Use instead
"We can't do that"	"Let me get some help to resolve this." "Is there someone (or something) else we can do?"
"I don't know"	"I'll find out." Customers expect us to know something!
"Sorry you'll have to ..."	"Here's how we can help you with that..." We're servicing the customer; the customer shouldn't have to do anything.

Most importantly, we never do anything to inconvenience

a customer. Being part of a "Yes" experience requires a "can do" attitude.

Great companies create fans by positively resolving inevitable problems.

*

We like to say that we make the customers feel special every day from the moment they walk through our front door and we greet them. Some days it's easier than other days. A woman dropped her car keys in a manhole outside one of our Commerce Bank stores, and a cashier climbed down and recovered them for her. Another time, a team member drove a customer to the airport when he was late for a plane.

And perhaps the number one Commerce customer service story of all time occurred in an inner city store in Camden, New Jersey. A customer was getting on a flight at midnight to go overseas, and as he was packing he realized he couldn't find his passport. As he retraced his steps, he realized that the last time he used it was as ID at a Commerce store to cash a cheque. But now it was 10pm, the store was not open, and the guy was sure that that was where he left his passport.

He called our call center, which is open 24/7/365, and a customer service representative took the call. She put him on hold and called her boss at home.

"What do you think I can do?" the rep asked.

"Ask him where we can reach him, and tell him to hang in there," the boss said. "We will figure it out."

The boss called the retail market manager for Camden and together they reached the assistant store manager. He, in turn, called the Camden police. The police met the assistant manager at the store and they went in together and found the passport.

This all happened rapidly, with less than 30 minutes between the time of the call and the point when the passport was located.

Meanwhile, we called the customer and he was instructed to pull up at the store's drive-thru window, where his passport was waiting, and he made his flight.

This actually happened to us *twice*. The other time was on a Sunday morning before opening hours. These are situations where we go outside the box to think about how the customer might feel and what we can do to help them.

Every day at Metro Bank, there are team members doing similarly Herculean tasks in the name of service.

*

Customers come in a wide variety of shapes and sizes, and they bring an equally wide variety of wants, needs, expectations, attitudes, and emotions with them.

Here are some things our team members do to make them all feel special:

- **Smile.**
- **Immediately give their undivided attention.**
- **Speak in a friendly tone of voice.**
- **Address external customers by name.**
- **Express a sincere desire to help.**
- **Say "Thank you!"**

Customer service depends on good communication: verbal and non-verbal. The words we speak, hear, or read are only a small part of how customers perceive us.

But what about what we're saying non-verbally? Are we still making the customer feel special?

Here are some non-verbal tips:

- **Stand.** By standing when we greet customers, we demonstrate a willingness and desire to assist.

- **Eye contact.** Making eye contact acknowledges that we see, and are dealing with, our customers as individuals.

- **Silence.** We can and do communicate even when we're saying nothing. Remaining silent while customers are talking is a basic courtesy; nodding tells them we're listening and understanding what we hear. Prolonged silence, however, can leave customers concerned. An occasional "I see" or "uh-huh" indicates that we're still listening, without interrupting.

- **Gestures.** Closed gestures such as tightly crossed arms, hands tucked deep in pockets, or clenched fists create non-verbal barriers. Open gestures invite people into our space and say we're comfortable having them near us.

- **Posture.** "Stand up straight," as mother always said, and she was right. Good physical posture conveys confidence and competence.

- **Overall appearance.** Look the part. Cleanliness and neatness communicate competence.

- **Facial expression.** We all know the cues: a raised eyebrow communicates surprise; a wink, sly agreement or alliance; tightly set lips, opposition; a wide-open smile, friendliness.

The customers that we make feel special will become special customers: fans.

*

Promises can and should be managed. Once we know what customers do and don't expect—they *always* expect us to keep our promises—we are in a position to shape customers' expectations to match what we can do for them.

Timeliness has always been important. Today, responsive and immediate action is even more critical. Businesses are creatively selling themselves on how they are able to get things done quickly:

- Federal Express—"Absolutely, Positively, Overnight"
- Pizza Hut—"5-Minute Meal Guarantee" (at lunchtime)
- Lens Crafters—"Custom-crafted eyeglasses in about an hour"

Being responsive means being able to set and *meet* deadlines. Deadlines are important. But deadlines are *created*. When we say to a customer, "I'll have it for you this afternoon," or "I'll mail it today," we are creating an expectation and setting a deadline for ourselves. Be realistic, because once created, deadlines become a yardstick by which customers measure your success or failure.

Create acceptable, realistic expectations of responsiveness for customers and meet those expectations.

＊

What we did at Metro Bank was to transport the American concept of community banking: we're here to service the customer.

In community banking, one person is the customer's banker. One person handles the relationship and the customer deals with that team member almost exclusively.

The British model—and, frankly, the US model at many large banks—is totally different. One person develops the business and hands it over to a second person, who underwrites it and makes the loan decision and hands it over to a third person, who handles the account going forward. It's called the "Finder, Grinder, Minder" model.

A real banker wants to handle the entire relationship. That's something the industry did successfully 30 years ago, but the banking model in both the US and the UK has slipped away from it.

Metro Bank doesn't put 25 hurdles between itself and its customers, forestalling a loan decision. The people they need to see to make a loan decision are on the premises every day. The credit people are there. Craig Donaldson, the Metro Bank CEO, is there.

We are local lenders making local loans.

We empower our Metro Bank team members as entrepreneurs, just as we did at Commerce Bank. By our definition, an entrepreneur has an ownership interest in the business. We convert our team members into entrepreneurs by sharing an ownership interest in the bank, not only because they might have bought stock, but also because they are incentivized through stock options. Stock options give team members the right to buy shares in the company at a fixed price, which means that as the market value of the company goes up, so does the value of their stock. The wealth creation at Commerce was a product of stock options and it motivated our team members monetarily, literally staking them to an ownership interest. All Metro Bank employees receive stock options, which—if the bank performs as we anticipate it will—a number of years down the road will create a lot of new wealth.

Metro Bank employees take a personal pride in their team membership that you won't see at other banks. At other banks, there's really no pride in going to work each day. It's just a job. Join Metro Bank and you're part of a model that is revolutionizing British banking. It's a service model where people come to work and enjoy themselves, which is why it is becoming more and more common to see Metro Bank team member pins being worn all over London. Customers recognize the big red "M" and smile at the wearer. They say, "Wow! You work for my bank, and you're obviously as proud of the affiliation as I am!"

It's just one more way we convert customers into *FANS*.

8

Dogs Rule and Kids Rock!

Histories are more full of examples of the fidelity of dogs than of friends.

Alexander Pope, 18th century poet, *The Rape of the Lock*

At Metro Bank, we throw out the welcome mat to our customers' dogs.

Some people might think our "Love Your Bank At Last" slogan is aimed at dogs. And we won't deny that.

You can bring your dog into our stores. Dogs have become members of the family—you wouldn't chain your children to the tree outside and leave them there, would you? We've got fresh water in the front entrance waiting for them. We'll give them free treats and a cool Metro Bank bandana to wear.

Why? Because if we love your dog, you know we love you, too.

Our initiatives are about being all the things that will make anyone feel like a loved and valued member of the Metro Bank community. We're the people who sponsor the local football team and we're there at all the times when you need us most.

On opening day at Holborn, the only people who brought their dogs in were the ones we personally invited. We were right there at the front door, Shirley and I, with our own pup, who is now known as Sir Duffield, "Duffy" for short. (He even has his own Twitter feed; follow him @SirDuffield.) Londoners had to see it to believe such behavior would be truly acceptable, no matter what they read in our ads and marketing literature.

We have dogs in the stores all the time, an emotional branding twist that is entirely due to Shirley's influence.

The story starts with what is now an embarrassing truth: I would never let our four children have a dog or a cat. I always thought of pets in terms of negatives: messy, noisy, disruptive, unpredictable. We had a rabbit for a month—only because Shirley and the kids hid him in the laundry room and it took me that long to catch on.

But when the last of our four children went off to college, Shirley informed me she had waited long enough.

"I'm getting a dog," she said.

"No, you're not," I said.

Let me cut to the chase: she got a dog, a Yorkshire terrier.

Our friends and associates, knowing my longstanding aversion to household pets, placed bets on how long it would be before the dog would be sleeping in our bed. I told them they were crazy to even suggest such a thing. It took three days.

As for Metro Bank's policy of not only allowing but encouraging dogs in our stores, it goes back to 2001 when we were preparing to open the first Commerce Bank stores in New York City and Shirley was in the city, shopping our soon-to-be competition, experiencing the practices of different banks. Duffy was with her at every stop.

At most banks, the guard would stop them at the front entrance. "I'm sorry," they would say. "No dogs allowed in here."

If she made it inside, somebody else would come rushing up and say the same thing.

Shirley, fed up, finally went outside and called our own bank's headquarters and asked for the compliance department.

"Do me a favor," she said, "please check the state and federal bank regulations and find out if there is something on the books that says that a dog cannot go inside a bank."

Three days later, our chief compliance officer called back. "We can't find anything," he said.

At that moment, "Dogs Rule!" was born.

*

In the UK, we're the official bank for the Kennel Club and we do weekend doggie adopt-a-thons with Battersea Dogs & Cats Home, which is world famous and is supported by the Royal Family.

Established in 1860, Battersea Dogs & Cats Home (www.battersea.org.uk) aims never to turn away a dog or cat in need of help. It reunites lost dogs and cats with their owners or cares for them until new homes can be found, giving them shelter and the highest standards of kenneling and veterinary care.

We met with the Battersea director and asked, "Have you ever thought about offering dog adoptions in a bank?"

"What?!?"

The brash and crazy Americans had struck again.

We explained our "Dogs Rule" policy and how we welcome canines in our stores in the UK and US. She, in turn, explained the admirable and detailed Battersea adoption vetting process in which the organization checks a family's credentials, interviews its children, sits with existing family pets and suchlike. It's wonderful how careful and considerate they are. Unfortunately, the process as it existed could take hours.

We made Battersea a proposal: if you can figure out a way to streamline the process, we'd like to do adopt-a-thons in our stores.

They accepted our invitation for a trial, two-day run at our Borehamwood store which we called a "Dogs Rule Weekend."

We made an event of it, hiring a DJ who played only dog-oriented songs such as *Who Let the Dogs Out?* and *How Much is that Doggy in the Window?* We hired a paw reader who read a dog's paw and told the owner what the dog was thinking. More than 25 families signed up to rehome a dog. And if they brought their current dog or adopted a new dog *and* opened an account we gave them a £20 bonus to put in the account.

Battersea's chief executive, Claire Horton, told the press:

> Battersea is thrilled to play a leading part in this exciting
> Metro Bank initiative. The bank are fantastic supporters of the
> Home and this is a great opportunity to take some of our dogs
> to meet everybody outside the kennel environment in the
> hope of finding them loving new homes.

The test was so successful that all our stores in the UK have regular adopt-a-thon weekends.

*

The Kennel Club is the largest organization in the UK devoted to dog health, welfare and training. Its objective is to ensure that dogs live healthy, happy lives with responsible owners.

The Kennel Club invests in welfare campaigns, dog training, and education programs and the Kennel Club Charitable Trust, which supports research into dog diseases and dog welfare charities, including Kennel Club Breed Rescue organizations that rehome dogs throughout the UK.

We are extremely pleased to be their official banking partner and to play our part in their Open for Dogs campaign. Metro Bank is all about convenience, and that is what we offer. You should not be forced to leave your dog outside banks that are supposed to be serving you. We're here to do things differently from other London high street banks.

Rosemary Smart, the Kennel Club's chief executive, said:

It is refreshing to see a new breed of bank, which recognizes that dogs are part of the family and incorporates that into its business policy.

Metro Bank even won an award in the Kennel Club's prestigious Open for Dogs Competition 2011. We were nominated by the public in the annual competition's London high street category, beating other well-known high street businesses to scoop this top award.

The Kennel Club's Open for Dogs campaign aims to break down barriers for man's best friend by encouraging more businesses to be dog-friendly. This is supported by research released by the Kennel Club which shows that a staggering four out of five businesses claim that their dog-friendly policy has helped them draw in more customers in difficult financial times.

Metro Bank's appreciation of its canine-loving customers paid off, as dozens of nominations flooded in to support the bank each day, helping us to beat the stiff competition. One member of the public who nominated Metro Bank commented on its "refreshing way of doing business," which helped to secure nominations.

Caroline Kisko, communications director at the Kennel Club, said:

> The winners of these awards are determined by the public, who recognize that Metro Bank is willing to go above and beyond for its customers and that dog-friendly businesses are an important part of the British high street. Metro Bank is a fine example of the many companies and organizations that are reaping the benefits of a dog-friendly door policy in terms of creating a welcome atmosphere, as well as helping to secure itself financially by widening its customer base.

The Kennel Club has found that 95 percent of people think more businesses and locations should be open for dogs, and that dogs improve the atmosphere of a place, and 77 percent think that dogs help to reduce stress.

*

Great brands become great community members. That's part of the reason Metro Bank UK also has a children's banking initiative called "Kids Rock."

It starts with a "5 for 5 Club" in which children under 11 open a savings account with £5 from us to get it started. We encourage them to return and make deposits of their own by providing a special club membership card and a plastic "M" bank to store coins in between visits. Each time they return, the kids get a prize and the card is punched. When they have been in the club for five months, we put another £5 in the account to celebrate. We want their trip to Metro Bank to be as anticipated and thrilling as a visit to McDonald's.

At 11, a youngster can have a Metro Bank savings account in their own name, which is an exciting day in many children's lives.

The "Metro Money Zone" educational program teaches kids about money, finance, savings, and the importance of making and sticking to a budget. We put together a sophisticated, accredited program in which we go into year 3 and year 4 classrooms for three sessions. The fourth session is held on site at the neighborhood Metro Bank.

We're passionate about what we do, so we believe we're well placed to spread that passion by sharing our knowledge of all things financial. Our Money Zone program works with schools in the community, giving children an understanding of the basic principles of money, saving, and banking in an engaging and fun way (and in line with the National Curriculum). The highlight is when the kids visit our stores, open their accounts, and become new fans.

Kids Rock at Metro Bank, which in simple terms means we value our younger customers and believe that banking should be made fun. Aside from the friendly and welcoming experience you'll get from visiting your local store, there's an array of fun stuff to enjoy: win prizes using our Magic Money Machine, enjoy free lollipops, save your coins in our M Banks, and much more. There are just so many reasons to visit!

Great brands become great community members.

Part 3

Culture Counts

9

Five Ways to Amaze

Be a yardstick of quality. Some people aren't used to an environment where excellence is expected.

Steve Jobs, co-founder, Apple

To create a great business, create a pervasive culture that executes a differentiated model. And fanatically execute to exceed expectations.

Our goal is to revolutionize British banking by creating fans not customers. And the number one customer principle that will take us there can be summarized in one word: AMAZE!

Here's how we spell it out and explain it.

A—Attend to every detail

Retail is in the detail, so make sure that your store always looks its best. Keep your facilities in pristine condition for customers to enjoy and appreciate. Are your marketing materials current?

Make sure that you attend to every detail of the customer experience, and that whatever issue you're dealing with is accurate. All it takes to scare off a new customer is misspelling their name once.

Here are some examples of how Metro Bank team members have attended to every detail:

- A customer came to Bromley to transfer his ISA and open a £50,000 fixed bond with Metro Bank. While waiting for credit references to approve and backdate the £50,000 bond, a customer service representative offered him a cup of coffee, then thought, "Why not offer him some biscuits, too?" Because he extended this simple courtesy, the customer cancelled putting the year's allowance into a Nationwide variable ISA and instead took out another ISA with us.

- A Metro Bank team member had a customer who only spoke Arabic. Unable to find another team member who could translate, he called several friends until he found one who could translate for him. He put the customer on the phone and was able to complete the desired transaction. The customer was AMAZEd and deposited £35,000 into a new account.

- A Metro Bank team member set up a loan for a customer who requested that the funds be dispersed in two weeks. In the meantime, the loan rate was dramatically reduced, from 10 percent to 7.9 percent. Realizing that this meant the customer was not getting the best possible deal, the assistant store manager told the team member to invite the customer back to the store so that he could receive the new rate—a saving of more than £420. The customer felt the team member had exceeded his expectations and returned to the store a third time to present her with a box of chocolates and a bottle of wine.

M—Make every wrong, right

To err is human and to recover is divine. So, if we *do* make a mistake—because we are human—we want to make sure that we apologize to our customer and also that we give them what we call a satisfaction guarantee. We put our money where our mouth is and if we make a mistake, we give customers money for it. *Apologize! Fix it right away!* And make sure that their satisfaction is guaranteed every time.

- When we had a processing problem with MasterCard, it came to our attention that a customer couldn't pay for their airline flights. A Metro Bank team member stepped in. She put the customer's flights on her *personal* credit card so that the customer could still take advantage of a good deal, and transferred the money—with permission, of course—from their account.

- One evening at 9pm, our IT system crashed and the call center was unable to access customer accounts or details. At that time, a customer called to transfer funds from his ISA to his current account. He explained that it was extremely urgent as he needed to pay a bill in the morning before leaving for work. A Metro Bank team member promised the customer that the payment would be made and said he would call him back as soon as the issue was resolved and the payment completed. An hour later, he called the customer to explain that the problem had not yet been resolved, but he would stay in the office until the system was back up. It was finally fixed at around 11.10pm. He contacted the customer the following morning to make sure he was able to withdraw his funds. The customer made a point of telling us how impressed he was that the team member had stayed on the job to see through the urgent transaction.

A—Ask if you're not sure, bump it up

At Metro Bank, it takes just one person to say "Yes" to a customer but *two* to say "No." So, if somebody has a request that a cashier or customer service representative or loan officer is not sure they can approve, we do not automatically say "No."

We "bump it up" to a supervisor. Then the supervisor and the team member come to a conclusion together. We empower our employees; if they feel that it's the right thing to do, they have the authority within certain guidelines to make decisions on behalf of the customer's welfare and benefit. But if they're not sure, they *ask*. Bump it up. Never say no at the first opportunity. Look for an alternative solution that leads to a "Yes!"

- At a training course a team member asked why self-authorization for a customer was capped at £5,000, when an ISA allowance is £5,000. This rule caused extra permissions to be sought every time. By bumping this up to our chief executive, who immediately changed the threshold, customers and colleagues have been saved a great deal of time and frustration.

- A customer was due to leave for holiday at midday on a Friday and he had not received a promised new debit card in the post. Team member Kim Van Der Berg spoke to both the Borehamwood store and the customer to try and remedy the situation. Unfortunately, the customer was busy at work and could not travel to another store to pick up a replacement. Kim bumped it up, printed the card at the Holborn store, arranged for a new PIN, and personally delivered the card to the customer at home that night.

Z—Zest is contagious, share it

Zest is all about behaviors. When you come in during the day, we want you to have a zest for your job that shows. We want you to be happy. We want your customer to see that you're happy. We want you to share that zest with everyone around you so the customer feels it from the second that they walk in, through their entire transaction and until the time that they leave. That's what makes us different.

- A customer service representative collapsed during

training and the paramedics were called. While she was in the ambulance, she told them about how good Metro Bank was and sent a fellow team member back to the store to make up goody bags for the paramedics who had helped her. At a later date, they all came back to the Kensington High Street store for a visit—and all opened accounts!

E—Exceed expectations

Exceed the *customer's* expectations. If a customer comes in and makes a deposit, instead of just giving them a receipt and saying, "Thank you very much," ask, "Is there anything else that I can do for you? Would you like the balance on your account?" Go the extra meter.

- An Uxbridge colleague noticed that a customer was about to go out in the rain in a lovely suit. She asked him if he'd like an umbrella and gave him her own to ensure he didn't get wet. He came back the next day to return the umbrella and deposited £10,000. But that wasn't the end of the story; he brought along several family members who all opened new accounts.

- Another customer came in to our Uxbridge store and explained that she'd been the victim of fraud: her account had been cleared. She had no cash on her and was worried about how she was going to pay for food for her family over the coming weekend. While several employees helped untangle her account and return its balance, other Metro Bank team members bought the customer several bags of food to ensure that her family did not go hungry.

- Croydon colleagues helped a customer whose handbag was stolen the day before she was due to leave on holiday. Staff kept the store open until the customer was able to get there at 8.45pm. They printed her a new card and ordered in food to share with the happy customer. They then walked her to her car and even paid her parking fee.

*

Successful, customer-facing businesses try to see things from the customer's point of view. Put yourself in the customer's shoes. Don't hide behind rules; don't hide behind policies.

Think about going out to dinner at a restaurant:

- Before you enter a restaurant, you evaluate it based on the location, the advertising and the look of the people who work there. Is the car park clean? Can you smell the aroma of good food or the remains of half-eaten meals in the dustbin?
- As you walk through the door, you make more judgments. Do the employees look friendly? Are you greeted at the door and made to feel welcome?
- During the meal you evaluate the items on the menu from how well the food is presented to how it tastes.
- Most importantly, how well are you being served? Kindly? Or with utter disinterest and contempt?

The best rule of thumb is never do or give something to a customer you would be embarrassed, reluctant, or angered to receive yourself.

*

What the public doesn't see inside our businesses is that we take the excellent customer service shown to external clients and apply its precepts internally as well.

Commerce Bank was home to "Dr. Wow," an imaginary character who uncovered and celebrated all the great things our people did for the public—and sometimes the things the public did for our employees in recognition of extraordinary service.

At Metro Bank, we've got "Major Amaze."

Once or twice a week, we hear a story in which our employees have exceeded a customer's expectations or something else really great has happened. Anyone can send a story in about anyone else or themselves. It's a process of reinforcing all the behaviors that we want from our employees. We don't do it every day because then it would become like wallpaper, so we pick out the best stories.

Here are some examples of moments Major Amaze has helped us celebrate at Metro Bank:

- During the Christmas holidays, several customers brought in biscuits and presents for the staff at the bank because they had been treated so well, such as when the staff kept the doors open late because somebody had to get something out of a safe deposit box.

- The Battersea Dogs & Cats Home took a picture of one store's staff because they love the service and everything we've done on our side of the partnership, and published the photo on *their* website. Major Amaze sent out an email telling all our employees about it.

- We've celebrated when an employee has gone above and beyond and taken an extra step to discover a "customer" trying to commit fraud and catching it before anything bad happened.

- We also have Major Amaze visits during which a team goes out to one of the stores and creates a big fuss around folk who have provided extraordinary service and gives them a reward. It might be a £25 or £50 gift card for their amazing effort.

Another way we recognize top service internally is a circle

of excellence dinner called "The Amaze Awards." People are nominated for recognition and our leadership team evaluates their success stories and then everybody votes. There is participation throughout all levels of the Metro Bank organization. All the nominees are invited and the winners are celebrated at a Metro Bank awards event.

At Metro Bank (and Petplan), our team members are rewarded for amazing customers and creating *FANS*.

10

Culture Counts!

Passion and standing up for things can help create a sense of unity. But you still have to act a certain way.

Arthur Blank, co-founder, The Home Depot

We have created a culture to match our model.

Anyone who has done business at or with Metro Bank—or collected a pay cheque from us—knows that we are different.

Culture—and recognition—was so important at Commerce that we had annual "WOW! Awards" to recognize our top-performing stores, reinforce our culture and reward our outstanding achievers—more than 8,000 of them each year. We didn't just put on a party hat to celebrate our success, we rented the legendary Manhattan Art Deco palace, Radio City Music Hall, and put on a gala show which included everything from a Commerce Bank team member talent show to the world famous Rockettes themselves.

Of course we do not do everything right. There will always be bumps in the road. But we keep and maintain our competitive advantage because we're not at the end; we have a long way to go.

So many people ask me, "How will we maintain the culture?," and I always say, "We are not in the maintenance mode." It is about *enhancing* the culture. It is about getting to the next level. It is about advancing the ball and staying ahead of the growth curve.

If you have a culture that wants to create fans and wants to have no stupid rules and wants to exceed customer expectations, *you will succeed*. But if you've got a culture driven only by making money, with a focus on getting costs down and driving productivity up, *you will not*.

You can try to cost-cut your way to prosperity, or you can grow your way to prosperity—obviously, we believe in the latter. Growth companies believe in their growth model and they invest and over-invest to grow their model and they create value through growth. Companies that do not have a growth model and try to cost-cut their way to prosperity rarely, if ever, succeed. At Metro Bank, for example, we overspend on buildings, on locations; we're open seven days, which is more expensive than weekday-only banking; and we make a substantial investment in call center design and training—although no customer will ever set foot there. We consistently over-invest for returns where our competition under-invests.

Many banks in the UK want to drive costs down, drive productivity up, and deliver modest customer service—but in *that* order.

What we want to create are fans, amazing service and convenience, and that is what we do. If you're trying to achieve great culture, great service, great convenience and to attract customers who will introduce other people to you, that's the basis for your decisions. If that's the core of everything you do, that's what you achieve. People look for a single silver bullet, but it's the million things you put together, and at the center of the million things is the culture.

Ultimately, the culture of Metro Bank is about our team members. We get fan mail every day, and that fan mail is never really about customers' current accounts or their online banking—it's about our people, about the heroic things that our people do that delight our customers with service. And it's about *FANS not customers*. One of the things we have been saying for a long time is that it is not just about meeting customers' needs or making customers satisfied, but about exceeding their expectations. We want to AMAZE them with service.

You may rightly wonder how much of this is just a different use of language—fans versus customers—and how much of it reflects the culture of the company.

It is *absolutely* about the culture of the company. We really think like retailers—not like bankers. If I had to categorize the traditional banking industry, it is low growth, low cost, low service, with an emphasis on product and price. Banking is a utility. The banks operate a low-cost model, for example outsourcing their call centers to India because it's cheaper.

Our response? *No way.*

Most banks are utilities that have no brand loyalty to you. No one is in love with a utility brand. Few people love BT (British Telecom). Does any American ever call Sprint for customer service? Think about it: there is something fundamentally wrong when a phone company can't or won't answer the phone.

The Old Guard manages from the expense side. It's all about mergers, acquisitions, and growth through acquisition. Service never enters the equation.

We operate an entirely different model: high growth, higher cost of operations based on wildly higher levels of customer service, and a focus on building brand and brand loyalties. There is nothing better than being able to create an emotional attachment to your brand, and that's done through customer service. It's that human element, that human contact. That's what makes *FANS out of customers*.

11

Hire for Attitude, Train for Skill

We are there to save money for consumers, not to sell them products they don't need … The key is not to make the sale. The key is to cultivate the customer.

Bernie Marcus, co-founder, The Home Depot

When I hire, the first question I ask is, "Are you really as committed as I am to win?"

One of our biggest challenges is to make sure we continue hiring the right people. Some people like the comfort of 9 to 5 hours, being told what to do, punching the clock, and not making waves. Most bankers have risen in an environment where, if you keep your head down and don't say the wrong thing, a job in banking is almost an entitlement. That's not the attitude *we* look for. Sometimes it takes a while to convince people that working harder than they ever have before, and being held accountable at a higher level than ever before, may be right for them.

"We train people differently at Metro Bank," says CEO Craig Donaldson. "We say their job is to go the extra mile. We reward them for traveling the extra mile and we make them feel special when they do something that creates fans. We recruit people who know what they want to achieve and that's great, great customer service. And that's not something that you put onto a recruiting poster. It's not something that you say. It's something you genuinely believe in and you genuinely live. And my job is to be the most extreme because I've got to be the one who leads this and makes sure that everybody knows that's what they have got to do."

He continues, "It's very simple. It's setting expectations and helping people feel good when they achieve them. We truly have a culture that wants to create fans and wants to do the right thing for customers. We keep the business of banking simple and focused on what it should be."

We believe in a simple hiring formula: if you've got the right attitude towards a job, we can teach you the skills. But if you don't have the right attitude for the fast-moving customer-centric culture that our growing bank represents, we can't teach you a thing.

When hiring for a wide array of customer-facing positions, we often prefer men and women who were not already in banking. Existing bankers often bring too many bad habits, too much baggage, too many stupid rules. We like retail people, folk who already put the customer first.

It is not uncommon for my wife Shirley or me to be out somewhere and receive extraordinary service, and then invite that person to call in about a job with us.

*

Hire for attitude, train for skill is our mantra.

If somebody walks in for a job interview and they don't smile within the first two minutes—we call it the "Smile Trial"—we don't hire them. Because if they want a job and they're walking in and not smiling, what in the world would make us think they will smile at a customer?

Great business models make good team members great. Our

job is to make sure that they have sufficient resources, tools, and knowledge to do a job and do it in an excellent manner. Training, learning, and continuous development are a huge part of achieving it.

We focus on the things that will make a difference in the customer service experience. This means making sure that our culture of excellence is spread through every single bit of training, that every single day we deliver, so that those messages are reinforced and our people truly do understand this culture of customer service excellence and performance excellence.

Not everybody can or should work at Metro. It is not a typical bank. It is a retailer providing financial products and services. That is what we do, so our job is to make sure that our customers walk away not just satisfied but very, very happy. Employees must understand clearly what our offering is, what our value proposition is, why customers should bank with us.

We sometimes get into trouble when an employee dealing with a customer problem he or she can't appropriately solve doesn't bump it up, or actually creates a stupid rule because the bank that employee came from had a rule for them to hide behind.

At Metro Bank, we're creating a new breed of proud people—customers and employees alike. At Commerce, people had an enormous amount of pride in working for the company because they knew, far and away, that we were the best.

If you have a cashier background, that's fine. But we look more closely at what you have done in the customer service area. Are you smart enough to learn our systems and gain knowledge? Then we put you through extensive training and you have to pass tests in order to make it to the front line. Once you get to the front line, you're observed once a month and given feedback.

The most important thing is having the right attitude, the right "can do" spirit. We want to make things better around you every day. We don't want you to just come into work and go home again in the evening. It's your attitude that's important. We can train you to deal face-to-face with customers, talk over the computer, answer the phone, and come up with the right things to say.

The "Hire for Attitude, Train for Skill" philosophy underpins our whole recruiting effort.

One of the things we have been able to do is develop a lot of people for the bank. As we grow into markets outside London they have the opportunity, if they want to relocate, to bring our culture to those new areas. We can complement the people we hire from these areas—areas that have what I call market equity—with people who really understand our culture and our brand.

*

As Metro Bank has grown in the UK, so has our training organization. (The original Commerce University, in New Jersey, was modeled on the Disney Institute; the Walt Disney folk invited us in and were generous with their advice in shaping our original corporate training center.)

We have constructed multiple Metro Bank University teaching facilities alongside certain stores to facilitate both new employee training and continuing education programs, so that we can grow the next generation of managers and leaders from within. The main facility is in Holborn, but there are many satellite centers to reduce travel time.

Classes are taught in person as well as online. And, unlike some organizations, we pay our team members their regular salaries while they attend Metro Bank classes.

Once hired, a new team member will go through the Visions and Values classes. Visions is an introduction to who we are. It's not about process or procedure or even products—it is about our past, our present, our future, and what makes us different. It is also the atmosphere in which new hires will learn the necessary behaviors to execute and deliver our brand of amazing customer service. It's also a fun day in which we want to get them excited to join the Metro Bank team so that they, in turn, will make our customers happy.

For cashiers and CSRs, Visions is followed by job training, which will entail several weeks of study and practice—in the classroom and later in the stores. That's the how-to. There are also ancillary computer courses in Microsoft Word and Excel.

On the continuing education side of Metro Bank University, we have a series of "Lunch and Learns," in which team members are invited to gather and talk to our chief executive, chief finance officer or other bank leaders on topics such as how our bank makes money or how team members can contribute to our further success.

The course offerings will expand and grow with the bank—in the pipeline are career development and mentoring programs.

*

One of my points of pride in Commerce Bank is the vast number of people who started at entry-level positions and grew with the business over the years. I want to share the stories of two of them: former Commerce University dean Rhonda Costello and former Commerce Bank senior credit officer Pete Musumeci.

Pete was instrumental in building the foundations within this company for the credit and credit culture side of the business. Pete is the rock. Both of them were instrumental in the creation of Metro Bank in the UK; Rhonda developed our training curriculum and Pete built the commercial lending program.

They are great examples of people who started in proscribed, supporting positions at a small company. As the company grew, the demands on them grew and they blossomed in ever changing jobs and roles as their responsibilities evolved and challenged their original assumptions of who they were and who they could become.

Commerce Bank rewarded Rhonda and Pete with options based on their performance, and the options had great value because of the success of the company. The same opportunities now exist at Metro Bank for a new generation of team members. The *number* of stock options you get depends on your performance. The *value* of the options over time depends on the success of the company as a whole. Because of that, everyone is working for the team instead of just their individual interests. Pete and Rhonda are two examples of how that happened and how they created major wealth.

But I'll let them tell you their Commerce Bank stories in their own words.

Rhonda Costello's story

When I came to Commerce Bank, we only had six locations. I started out as a store manager. A little more than a year or so later, Vernon started to grow the bank and the culture as well. I was fortunate enough to be selected to become one of the first three regional vice presidents in the company. I was responsible for deposit growth, customer service, loan growth, and fee income for the stores and lending officers in my region. I had never made a commercial loan in my life and Pete Musumeci taught me how to do that. I held that role for several years then the bank started its rapid growth.

Vernon then asked me to become the HR director and make the recruitment function run like a business line. What a learning curve that was, going from the sales side to HR and the corporate structure. It was also extremely exciting because we had started up two new divisions: insurance and capital markets. I was involved in creating and getting them on board and promoting the culture, making sure everybody understood the Commerce Way.

The learning curve was as steep as you could possibly imagine, but it was a great, great experience for me as a young woman. It also raised a new issue for me: did I want to spend my career in the back office or did I want to be on the front line?

I raised my hand and went to talk to Vernon about it. He said, "Keep doing what you're doing and I have something new in mind for you. I'll be back to you when it works out." Within a month, he decided to expand from New Jersey into the state of Delaware and to start to build branches there. He asked me if I would head up the Delaware operation and get our stores up and running there. I said yes.

Six months later, at a branch opening, Vernon walked up to me and said, "Ah, just the woman I want to talk to." He said that we were acquiring a bank in Northern New Jersey. Would I be interested in handling the conversion of their systems and culture into ours? Once again, I said yes. I was there within a week and handled that.

A year later, I answered the phone and it was Vernon wanting to know if I would be willing to do it all over again with another acquisition. I said sure and we grew those next seven locations into 22 within two years. We were really busy, but I'm telling you, we had such a great time.

The next time he called, Vernon asked if I would be interested in going to Pennsylvania, which—with 40 stores—was the largest market that we had at the time. They needed someone with my retail background and we grew our presence in the state from 42 to 73 stores.

In every role, in every new market we entered, I learned our model worked just as well as it had before.

At that point, I was interested in getting back into the corporate side of things at Commerce. The head of Commerce University, our in-house training operation, announced plans to retire. I had taken a lot of banking and leadership courses over the years, so I was asked to become the new dean of Commerce University.

That was one of the best experiences, building culture and team members. During my time, we built a new main campus university and grew to 22 satellite campuses.

When Vernon began in London, I helped take the methods, processes and ideas over. My goal was to build our training methods, build our culture, and teach our new team members to create fans. I worked to be sure the culture was understood, and made sure the buzz was there. My job was to coach executive management. We also trained the team in grand openings, which are really a theatrical performance in many ways. The culture starts at Metro Bank University. All the learning and development, all the culture, have to be woven into it. We offer Visions and Values classes, cashier and CSR training, leadership, technical and some other classes.

People like to be treated well. People are tweeting on Twitter about how great this bank is. They are opening up new accounts in droves. They tell us we have made banking enjoyable.

My story is hardly unique. I can tell dozens, maybe hundreds of stories about Commerce Bank employees just like myself who started in entry positions and grew with the company. They began as part-time cashiers or customer service representatives in the call center, worked hard, recognized the wealth of opportunities that rampant growth brought, took advantage of job training opportunities and rose to management and leadership roles with commensurate salary and benefits such as stock options.

I built my first house with the money I earned from Commerce Bank stock options. I got all these options along the way because of my performance. The value of the options depended on the performance of the company as a whole and because of that I created major wealth. It was really quite amazing. It afforded me such a better lifestyle than I and my family would have had otherwise. At Commerce Bank—and now at Metro Bank—Vernon always shares the wealth.

Pete Musumeci's story

I was born and raised in Swedesboro, New Jersey. When I graduated from Manhattan College in Riverdale, the Bronx, in 1972, I moved back home and went to work for the local bank in Swedesboro. Two years later, I started with Commerce.

I began as a junior loan officer, primarily making consumer loans. I always reported to Vernon directly—not just then but for my entire career. He was the senior loan officer, but as I progressed under him, I rose to senior lender. In 1991, the bank had reached a size at which we needed to split that role in two, and I became the newly created senior credit officer.

In the years that followed, if there was a position open, Vernon wasn't afraid to put somebody who was less experienced in it. If he really believed in that person, and he saw skill and talent levels that impressed him as well as a strong work ethic and commitment to the Commerce culture, he wasn't afraid to let them grow into the job—he certainly did that with me. That's one of the best things I can tell you about my 30-year Commerce journey. He always seeks out the person whose potential matches up with an opportunity.

He would take a chance with them and see if they could grow into it. I later did the same thing when I filled positions. With an organization like ours, understanding the culture and how we do business are equally important. There's a lot to be said for somebody who has a pretty good understanding of that culture, and putting them in a position where they're not quite ready and let them grow into it because they have the necessary intangibles. The culture is ingrained in them. They work in it. They understand it and recognize its unique characteristics, as opposed to somebody from outside the organization who may have all the technical skills, but does not have the intangible understanding of the culture that an insider has.

I went to London to help create the commercial side of Metro Bank. My job was to instill our commercial and lending culture with relationship banking. We've taken a world-renowned model and shown that it works anywhere. It's a continuation of all the great things Commerce was about, redoing them in a new market: service, people dealing with people, relationship banking. It's not one of these sophisticated models that get all the big banks in trouble. Every customer we talk to in London says this is what they want, this is the way they want banking to be. This model is very, very portable.

At Commerce—and now at Metro Bank—if you can grasp what the culture is about and if you can get your arms around it, there's no ceiling to where you can go with it.

As far as the wealth that I made over the years working at Commerce, ultimately it all came down to the stock options and the growth of the company. Many, many people made a lot of money from those stock options—and when I say *a lot*, I mean *a lot*—and I was one of them. I changed and grew as my job changed and grew. I learned to do things I never dreamed I could when I joined the company—including helping Vernon create and build an entirely new bank, Metro, in London. I'm an example of a guy whose job evolved and who grew to meet it. And because of that, my responsibilities kept widening over the years and I created great wealth.

*

On the commercial banking side of staffing it's somewhat different, because when we're hiring lenders, we expect them to have a certain amount of lending and credit experience. The level of skill they bring with them depends on the position that we're offering, such as a real estate or health care lender, or whether it requires the ability to analyze credit relationships. Still, even lender candidates must have the Metro Bank attitude. They have to embrace our corporate, lending and credit culture.

You could be knocking the shine off the ball as a business

development person, but if you're not exhibiting the core competencies that we have decided as an organization we want to have, you may score an "A" in your production, but you'll rate a "D" in your competencies because you're not doing it the right way. These characteristics are all taken seriously at Metro Bank.

In some cases, it becomes a challenge because someone who previously worked in a different bank will say, "This is the way I used to do it." However they did it, *we* don't do it that way.

It's even more urgent when we hire people who are the equivalent or maybe a little bit higher than our store managers. "This is the way that we used to do it at Barclays." That's nice, but you're not going to get all your leads for business development at Metro Bank from somebody to whom you have to pay a fee.

People need to understand that our value proposition is "go out and sell it." Why would we pay a lead-generation fee to somebody else when we can walk straight into a business, talk to an owner or manager, and convince them that we have a better way?

Joining Metro Bank is all about breaking those bad habits, erasing all the stupid rules to which they were accustomed.

*

During the 11 years that Steve Jobs was exiled from Apple (1985–96), he led NeXT Computer and eventually acquired what became Pixar from George Lucas for a pittance—the sale of the century in Hollywood. That time eventually proved extremely profitable financially, but before that happened, Jobs still had a great deal to learn about how business works and where opportunity sometimes hides. He told biographer Walter Isaacson:

> When I went to Pixar, I became aware of a great divide. Tech companies don't understand creativity. They don't appreciate intuitive thinking, like the ability of an A&R guy at a music label to listen to a hundred artists and have a feel for which

five might be successful. And they think that creative people just sit around on couches all day and are undisciplined, because they've not seen how driven and disciplined the creative folks at places like Pixar are. On the other hand, music companies are completely clueless about technology. They think they can just go out and hire a few tech folks. But that would be like Apple trying to hire people to produce music. We'd get second-rate A&R people, just like music companies ended up with second-rate tech people. I'm one of the few people who understands how producing technology requires intuition and creativity, and how producing something artistic takes real discipline.

This ties in with my theory that people reinvent things. People who succeed are lucky that their job uses their special unique talent. We brought high-impact retailing into the banking business, first at Commerce and now at Metro Bank. Jobs said that the tech companies and the music companies never talked to each other until iTunes came along. Similarly, bankers and retailers were never on the same page before Commerce and Metro Bank brought them together.

If you fit the culture of a company and have the necessary technical skills and appropriate work ethic, your potential to grow in a company such as Metro Bank could be unlimited. It's obviously governed by the growth and needs of the company, but we always prefer to promote and hire from within.

One of things that affects promotion from within is whether there is somebody readily available to replace *you*. What have you done to grow your own successor? That's your responsibility and something unique within smart companies. If you want to move up, we need to replace you, and we prefer to do that from within, so what have you done to accelerate the process?

We have always told people that ours are entrepreneurial companies. "It is *your* company and we want you to look at it as if it was your company." The way people really made money at Commerce in particular was with stock options, so it was important that they understood our culture.

Employees can look around at any one of our companies and see numerous examples of people who were promoted from within.

The rapid growth we experienced at Commerce a decade ago is already taking shape at Metro Bank, and there are an enormous number of advancement opportunities for men and women who recognize it. Already, people have been promoted to leadership roles and unexpected jobs. They started out as cashiers and CSRs and have moved on to store administration and store operations. Those who work really hard are the ones who have been moving up within the company. Some have moved into the call center and become supervisors. Others have moved from the front lines of the stores to marketing.

You need a high level of integrity to work in our companies and you must play well with others because we don't want any type of political environment—it just gets in the way. When we go out and sell, we're selling Metro Bank. We're selling ourselves and how we are different. We can customize solutions for our customers. We're nimble. We're here for our customers. Neither employees nor clients will get caught up in a lot of red tape. We can make decisions very, very quickly, internally and externally. If that's the kind of service you want as an employee or a customer, we're the business for you.

Achieve your potential—that's exactly what we do for people. We're constantly looking for team members to work alongside us who can appreciate that and dream that. Such people are few and far between, but we've been incredibly fortunate in being able to get a team behind us who can see it and who believe it.

12

Hope is Not a Plan

If anyone is going to destroy our online shopping business model, it's going to be us.

Jeff Bezos, founder, Amazon

If anyone is going to reinvent British banking, it will be us—not because we hope it will happen but because we have the culture and the model, and are fanatical about execution.

People say to me, "I hope I get this deal." Or, "I hope she comes to work for us." "I hope he takes our loan commitment." "I hope we make our budget."

The list of declarations that start "I hope" goes on forever and I always end up saying, "Let's not hope about it. Go out and *make* it happen."

When people use the word *hope*, they're basically saying they don't have a plan. What I want to know is how are *you* going to make something happen? As a business plan, hope is not at all useful. We want to recruit people where hope is not a plan.

Don't dream about execution—*execute*!

We understand who we are, what we are and what we can accomplish. In other words, we don't *think* we're going to do something, we *know* we are.

Here's a relevant thought on this subject from Larysa Slo-bodian, a blogger and principal consultant at L4 Leadership: "It is wonderful to have hope, but hope is not a plan and cannot dictate change on its own. And, sometimes, hope can be the undercover agent for denial."*

What gets measured gets done! That has a lot to do with the building up of pipelines for new customers on both the retail and commercial sides of Metro Bank. When we talk about reporting and holding our people accountable, it means talking to them regularly. What else do you need? Do you need someone higher up to come in and help you close this deal? Do you need the chief executive to meet a client? Because let me tell you, being able to deliver that is incredibly powerful in our business. When we walk around at an opening and talk to people for hours and hours, we hear it's an access to the top not available at the main London high street banks. At Metro Bank, our customers will see the founder and CEO of the bank quite often.

If an account officer says, "If we do this loan, we *hope* to get all of the customer's deposit business," that's not the right approach. It should be, "If we do this loan, we *will* get all the deposit business."

We have great products, we have great people, we have great locations, so to the physical extent that we are able to handle the customer's deposit needs, we must believe we will get *all* the business, not just "hope" to get all the business.

We need a have a realistic basis for believing that our model will produce more business, not just "hope" it's going to produce more business.

*

---

* "When Does Rescue Turn Into Recovery?", February 10, 2011, L4 Leadership blog by Larysa Slobodian, www.l4leadership.com/14/executive/when-does-rescue-turn-into-recovery/

Hope is not a plan. You've got to plan and you've got to put the right things in place to deliver it. You've also got to base your plans in fact and in delivery and that's what we do.

Somebody will say, "I went to see a customer and I'm hoping they're going to come back to me."

And I'll say, "What have you done since then? When are you going back to them? Why would the customer have to come back to you? It's your job to make their life easier. How does them coming back to you make their life easier?"

"They wanted to think about it. They said they'd get back to me."

"So your plan is that you hope they'll get back to you? Hope is a plan now, is it?"

In the real world of chasing and developing business, you've got to have a realistic plan. You've got to take ownership and think, "How can I make life easy for customers?" That's the key.

We see this on both sides of the bank, consumer and commercial. Businesses need help; they need things to happen for them. Things certainly happen *to* them.

*

We're always looking to improve.

We took our original retail bank and we grew it every year in the US. Then we took the central model to a completely different market an ocean away and, lo and behold, it is a gigantic success because the principles are universal for successful retail businesses.

Every successful business must eliminate "hope" from its vocabulary and install execution and success in its place. Entrepreneurs make things happen; they don't wait for miracles.

There are plenty of differences between American business practices and those of the British. And there's no doubt that the "can do" American culture clashes with the "let's study it" British approach. The London media and business establishment asks us all the time why there has not been a new bank in Britain in more than 100 years. I could be diplomatic and lie or I could tell the truth.

The real answer is a reluctance to challenge the status quo.

In our job interview process at Metro Bank (and Commerce before), certain candidates will move up the ladder and meet a variety of officers and executives, depending on the vacancy. At some point, someone will ask the candidate, "Do you understand the Metro culture? Do you understand the lending culture and the credit culture and all that?" They invariably say, "Yes" and we will invariably say, "No, you don't." You don't have any idea what it's all about until you've been here and you've lived it and breathed it.

When you hire, does the applicant understand and buy into your model and culture?

A lot of men and women come to us from banks where the only way they could compete for customers was on price, whether that means interest rates, loan structure, loan terms or accepting a lack of guarantees. They could compete only by making it easier for the customer, compared with what other banks were offering. That's not how *we* compete. We never compete on price and we never compete on credit standards. We compete on everything that we do: the entire service mentality; the way every corner of the Metro Bank business works together; how we have an account officer who handles all of a customer's needs; how we will introduce the customer to the credit officer, senior management, or the local branch manager.

Many job candidates come to us believing that shaving half a point off a customer's existing rate or extending a loan by four years will close loans. We're not built that way. We compete on service, service, service and everything that means.

We ask the candidate, "Have you heard anything different from the four or five people you spoke to?" And the answer is always "No" because we all do the same things the same way for the same reasons. We're consistent in our beliefs and our actions.

The word "control" is important at Metro Bank. How do we control the relationship? What's the hot button for the customer? What do they really need? What do they really want?

When we have control of the relationship—and we don't mean control in the sense that we will tell a customer how to run their business—when we understand what they need, we're positioning them to succeed because of the way the bank can help them. At times, that might mean saying "No" because the bank can't do something, or maybe what the customer wants isn't the right thing. They might not realize it, but maybe it isn't the right path or choice. When we have that kind of control of the relationship, it helps to solidify things and get business done a lot quicker and smarter.

We've been consistent for 35-plus years in the firm belief that *hope is not a plan*. Don't merely hope things will work out—have a real, executable plan of action!

*

Many of the British citizens we've met are a little bit like New Yorkers: skeptical!

When we first went into New York and announced that Commerce would be open seven days a week, Gothamites were dubious. "Okay," they said, "that will last six months, tops." And they reserved judgment for good reason: previous banks had not lived up to what they said they would do. Even the ones that tried to copy us by saying "We're going to extend our hours and be open on Saturdays in some locations" ultimately backed off.

When we really do what we say we will do and are consistent about our commitment to convenience and loving our customers, they love us unconditionally and become fans. And then they tell their friends. As everybody knows, the best recommendation is a one-to-one when somebody says, "Oh my, the bank just screwed that up again for you? Switch to my bank!"

*

At the opening of the first Metro Bank store in Holborn, people would come in tentatively, ask some questions, take some literature, and come back later to open an account.

As the next few stores opened, we saw that behavior evolve. Now people were bringing a passport and/or a rent statement or whatever they had that proved their residency. They were ready to do business immediately. They might say "Tell me more about Metro Bank," but they were sitting down at a team member's desk to open an account while asking their questions.

In the latest stores that we've opened, they're on their mobile phones before walking out with their new cheques and debit cards, calling their friends and telling them to come over and join them. I have seen the same person come back three times during an opening weekend, each time bringing more friends and family.

Metro Bank is catching on in London even quicker than Commerce did in Manhattan. After two years, we're hearing the same thing we did at Commerce: "When are you going to be in *my* neighborhood?"

13

Design as a Competitive Weapon

Design is the fundamental soul of a human-made creation that ends up expressing itself in successive outer layers of the product or service.

Steve Jobs, co-founder, Apple

Go ahead: judge our bank by its cover.

According to Walter Isaacson, author of the biography *Steve Jobs*, Apple stores average 5,400 customer visits a week. That's a stellar number for any retailer.

But if that's great business traffic, consider *this* number: Commerce Bank stores everywhere averaged 12,000 customers a week in 2006!

Our store is our public face. Metro Bank, and our lifeline to the customer, is the official reincarnation of the fans not customers model for banking and we know it will reach explosive traffic numbers in short order.

Like me, Jobs believed the best places for his retail stores were always the highest trafficked locations available. He believed the Apple stores should be in high-end malls and on high streets, areas with a lot of foot traffic, no matter how expensive the cost per square foot. He and I both believe the best site is almost always worth the price.

"We may not be able to get them to drive ten miles to check out our products, but we can get them to walk ten feet," he told Walter Isaacson. Microsoft Windows users, in particular, had to be ambushed. "If they're passing by, they will drop in out of curiosity, if we make it inviting enough, and once we get a chance to show them what we have, we will win."

Jobs went on to say, "In most people's vocabularies, design means veneer. It's interior decorating. It's the fabric of the curtains or the sofa. But to me, nothing could be further from the meaning of design. *Design is the fundamental soul of a human-made creation that ends up expressing itself in successive outer layers of the product or service.*" (Emphasis added.)

At Commerce, and now at Metro Bank, the look and the location and the design of our stores are a direct reflection of the brand and are an important element in communicating the brand. I picked all the locations at Commerce and do the same at Metro Bank. Shirley and her team design the facilities to reinforce the brand.

I don't have much design talent, but I know what I like. So while I might be the keeper of the brand, Shirley is the keeper of the look. You can see her touch in the big things, like the design of our buildings, inside and out. But it's also found in a multitude of smaller things, from desks and door handles to pens and dog bandanas. I couldn't have created the culture, look, and feel of these businesses without her substantial involvement and contributions.

Successful retailing is all about minding the details. How your store looks inside, how the products and services are presented, how your people look—these are all part of your brand. We constantly look at the height of ceilings, lighting levels, even how to best use the store floor itself. There isn't one thing in the presentation of the Metro Bank brand that wasn't thought about, from what you see every step up to and through the front doors. What can you see? Is it fun?

Shirley's entire career was fashioned around the ideas of Frank Lloyd Wright: design from the inside out. Her winning approach comes from knowing who will occupy a building and then making it a point of destination for that particular client from the outside: the signage, the materials, what the building itself looks like and how it looks on the site. But then, from the inside, she focuses on how it will operate. She feels that the culture of a business is innate and could be affected by its environment.

Shirley once created a large call center headquarters for Travelers Indemnity Company in the US. She insisted that it should be glass enclosed, and that it should not have low ceilings and terrible lighting—all common, low-cost approaches to such facilities. Her concept was that it should be one of the *best* places environmentally, not an oversized closet, because when Travelers employees picked up the phone to answer a customer's call, all the company had going for it was the representative's voice and attitude. She made the case that their attitude could be shaped by their surroundings, how they feel about themselves and the space in which they're working.

At Metro Bank, bringing ATMs inside the vestibules was a conscious decision. We couldn't put them outside, although we could have put a little roof over the machines. The reason they are inside is because we want to draw customers in to see the bank. If they aren't already customers, we want them to be AMAZEd! All the posters around the ATM signal Metro's convenience and the extended hours that it's open. If the ATM is safe and convenient, think how good the rest of the Metro Bank experience must be!

Customer service is a life's work. I learned, over the years, to trust Shirley's judgment, knowing that she would accurately interpret the look and feel of our brands. She knows—even when I don't. She knows the secret recipe: which colors are happy and which are drab; why one thing is round over here and has an angle over there.

Sometimes you can spot Shirley's touch in the tiniest details—like the millions of free Metro Bank pens we give away at every opportunity. She and her InterArch team even won an award for their design of a water bottle during the Commerce days.

As for pens, most banks go to great lengths to chain theirs to desks and counters so customers can't steal them. Why? We have always wanted customers to *take* our brightly colored pens, embossed with the Metro Bank logo. Need one? It's yours. Need five? Share them with your friends and, along the way, help us spread our name around. Talk about making an impression!

When Shirley and her staff designed the pens, they considered their weight, how they looked and how they felt. We didn't pick one out of a catalogue; we designed them from the inside out.

*

Retail design is more important than it ever has been because we are visually bombarded with information every second of every day.

We want you to know when you walk through Metro Bank's doors or encounter us via a brochure or an event that life is different at Metro. The experience is everything.

We place large sheets of street-facing glass in our store windows that let customers see in, in brightest day or darkest night. We think our stores look better at night than they do in the daytime because you can really see inside at night. They're open and architecturally carved by the lighting. The finishes are all high-end. It's impossible to look in our windows or walk through our doors without seeing people smiling.

There are local planning ordinances in some commercial areas of London that prohibit banks. They want retail because retail drives footfall. Traditional British banks have limited hours, they're dirty, they're not attractive, and they don't drive anybody onto a block or into a mall. But now that they see what we do, these same municipalities and developers are coming to us saying, "We've got this premier site, would you consider building a bank on it?"

*

As I have for the past 35 years, I turned to my wife Shirley to develop our Metro Bank and Petplan brands, and streamline them to go national and international.

In the UK, Shirley is doing even more at Metro than she did at Commerce. She directs the architectural design and the construction, but she is also the marketing leader and keeper of the brand.

Design is one of the core business basics at Metro Bank, from the bright red color that represents the brand everywhere you find it, to the big windows and the architectural lighting in the stores, day or night. Our desks are wood, not laminate, because that's where the customer sits, sending a clear message about how we feel about them. The flooring design is functional—*directional*—guiding customers in and about.

We started designing Metro Bank locations from the entry point, and it's a fun process, quite energizing. The focus is on thinking about someone else rather than ourselves.

The environment is crucial. It's not one thing, it's the sum of all the parts that creates the customer experience. When I walk through the door is the space open, is it friendly, is it bright, is it inviting? Is everything in excellent condition? Is there any clutter making things look messy? Does someone walk up and smile at me and say "Hello" and welcome me? When they give me a tour of the store and listen to my concerns and needs, do they know which product or service will improve my life? When I leave, am I thanked for my business?

The idea is to create a customer for life. If we fail on a lot of these components, we won't have that customer for life, will we? The way we continue to service that customer on a day-in and day-out basis is what makes us winners.

If you think about it, it's not too hard to figure out how you would *like* to be treated in a bank, and that's what Shirley is great at doing. You don't want to wait in line forever; you want the store to be open when you can get there. And the Metro Bank logo is seen behind the cashiers so you know without a doubt where you are.

Any successful retail business develops a unique, engaging, and fun environment. That is what turns customers into fans—every time.

14

No Stupid Rules

As a company, one of our greatest cultural strengths is accepting the fact that if you're going to invent, you're going to disrupt. A lot of entrenched interests are not going to like it. Some of them will be genuinely concerned about the new way, and some of them will have a vested self-interest in preserving the old way.

Jeff Bezos, founder, Amazon

What is a stupid rule?

Every organization has endless stupid rules. This is often an unintended result of the bureaucracy that is built up to support the business. Stupid rules are a result of misguided or erroneous assumptions about what best serves—or protects—an organization's status quo.

To this day, bankers tell me that I am nuts: "You shouldn't be open on Sunday, you can't be open on Sunday, because how do you hire people to work on Sunday?"

Let's see, every mall is open on Sunday, every retailer is open on Sunday, but bankers believe that there should be some mystique about running a branch bank. That, my friends, is one stupid rule!

Say you work for a company that has an account at a major bank, and you get paid with a cheque from that bank. If you don't have an account there, when you go in to cash your cheque, they might fingerprint you *and* charge you a fee. Does that make sense?

Here's what happened. The bank had a committee where some career banker said, "We can raise £50 million next year by charging £5 for this check-cashing service!" Can't you just picture the committee members rubbing their hands with glee? Then someone from security piled in: "We'll have to fingerprint all these non-customers to cut down on the fraud!"

But *nobody* raised a hand and said, "What will these actions do to the customer experience?" Because you and I know that if they fingerprint you once, you will *never* open an account at that bank. Nobody seems to appreciate what these inept policies do to the brand.

One of the things we did throughout the years at Commerce and now do at Metro Bank is to make sure that when we deliver a new product, whatever policies, procedures, and products we create are based on a simple standard. If we can't explain it to our 18-year-old team members, it's too complicated.

This is a non-banking view of life. Bankers want to create an aura about the industry because—stand back and prepare to genuflect in our direction—we are handling people's money. It's all bull.

It goes back to the essence of Sam Walton, who founded the world's largest, most successful and most profitable retail operation, Wal-Mart. In the retailing business, you don't have to be 100 percent better. You have to be 15 percent better, and you have to get better all the time.

Here are some of my favorite examples of other stupid British bank rules:

- **To open a new account, a bank requires a valid driver's license, passport, utility bills, etc!** If you're British and you have a valid driver's license or passport, that's all you need at Metro Bank for instant account opening. But at many British banks, you have to come back with your utility bills, the lease on your flat, plus a driver's license and/or passport. We eliminated that. We have machines that can validate passports and let us know immediately whether they're genuine or not. We put this technology in place to protect ourselves, yet the net result is convenience for our customers.

- **Make an appointment if you want to open a new account!** Requiring new customers to make an appointment to apply for a current or savings account is a stupid bank rule. Not only can you walk into a Metro Bank seven days a week and open a new account on the spot (including online banking), we even have "Bank at Work Days" in which we go to the workplaces of our business clients and sign up their employees for new accounts on the spot.

- **Allow two weeks to issue and/or replace debit and credit cards!** When a private banking customer of one of the big London high street banks lost his wallet just before leaving on holiday, he was surprised to find it would take his bank two weeks to replace his debit and credit cards. That would wreck his plans. Someone told him that Metro Bank could print new cards for a customer in any of its stores so he went into one and opened a new account. He left with new cards and a smile on his face. When he returned from his holiday, he transferred *all* his accounts to Metro Bank.

- **All loans must go through the pricing committee!** Some banks in Britain have what they call a "pricing" committee that determines whether a prospective loan is priced properly. Why do I need a committee of people to tell me if a loan is priced properly? Our account officers or credit people know our model and should be able to determine instantly whether we've got a loan priced properly.

- **No bikes in the bank!** For many reasons, our stores are designed to avoid entry stairways. Craig Donaldson, CEO of Metro Bank, discovered how convenient that is early one morning when he encountered a cyclist in one of the stores. The cyclist used to ride past our store every morning on the way to work when he noticed two things: (1) we're open earlier than any other bank in the neighborhood, and (2) because there are no steps at the store's entrance, he could ride his bike in, lean it against the counter, do his business and be on his way. Elsewhere, he'd waste time and energy chaining up his bike outside, doing his banking inside, going back outside, unchaining his bike and going. It's a small thing to a non-cyclist, but it takes time and it mattered to him. He said, "It's brilliant for me. Fantastic."

- **No toys for children whose math isn't perfect!** A little girl who must have been about four poured loose change into the Magic Money Machine but guessed the amount she entered incorrectly. She started crying because she couldn't have a toy. Of course, we gave her the toy because we want a happy child. The parents were blown away. They said that would have never happened at another bank: "They would have stuck to the rules." The cashier said, "Probably, but we don't want anybody unhappy."

The last story reinforces our "One to say yes, two to say no" rule. It's about our people doing the right thing. Or, more obviously, not doing stupid, detrimental things.

The CSR who came to the little girl's rescue told Craig, "In my previous bank I wouldn't have been allowed to do that because she hadn't guessed the right number."

"But she was crying," Craig said. "Wouldn't they just want to make her happy? Wasn't that the right thing to do?"

And she said, "Of course it was, but the process said you had to guess within £2. In my previous bank, I would have been reprimanded: 'Why did you do that? She didn't get it right!' Whereas here I knew it was the right thing to give her the toy, so I did."

And that's the difference. Can you imagine that family with the little girl going home, and the next day her dad telling parents at her school the story? You *know* they talked about it. Or the guy with the bike saying he told all his mates who cycle that they should do their banking at Metro as well. Oh, and if they leave wet or muddy marks on a rainy day, we'll wipe them up. It's not hard to do! Tell me where we lost a penny making these customers—I mean *FANS*—happy!

One of our favorite stories about killing a stupid rule was to do with Commerce Bank delivery vans. Why does every retailer paint their van with their marketing message and brand, but banks don't?

In most banks the security department is so worried about protecting the dead cheques they transport in unmarked vans that they give up tens of millions of advertising impressions a month by not painting their vans. The dead cheques have no cash value! They have to be physically moved from place to place for electronic scanning and regulatory fulfillment, but then they are destroyed. That's why we turned our fleet into brightly colored mobile billboards.

When I tell the vans story, bankers and non-bankers alike look at me. I ask them, "Do you paint yours?"

"No—the guys in security are afraid of letting us do it." If you won't paint your vans, what *will* you change?

Processes should be followed where they work. Where they don't, they should be challenged as stupid rules.

So many times, good ideas are struck down because they are too hard to execute. "No, they'll never do that, are you kidding?" Can't you just hear a business's operational people saying that?

Some people hear our "No Stupid Rules" philosophy and choose to bank with us for that alone.

Every business should pride itself on running a never-ending campaign to find and kill every stupid rule.

15

Petplan: Insurance for Our Four-Legged Friends

> The most important thing in life is to stop saying I wish and to start saying I will. Consider nothing impossible, then treat possibilities as probabilities.
>
> Charles Dickens, author, *David Copperfield*

The Metro Bank story is one of offering major value, achieved by creating a differentiated model enthused with a unique culture and delivered with fanatical execution.

What if I told you that we also applied *FANS not customers* to a completely different industry, one previously held in such low esteem it made bankers look good?

Bernie Marcus and Arthur Blank reinvented home improvement retailing. Steve Jobs did the same for computer, mobile phone and tablet sales. IKEA did it for low-cost, high-quality furniture. If we can do it for retail banking, what's stopping *you* from reinventing *your* business?

Petplan USA is another great example of our philosophy and execution at work. Two British entrepreneurs fulfilled their American dream by creating a new model for pet health insurance in the US by applying the New Math.

Chris and Natasha Ashton have created *FANS not customers*

at America's number one pet health insurer by redefining the business and creating a new model and major wealth.

Although hugely popular and successful in Europe, the pet insurance industry struggled mightily in the US market. The American company that pioneered the industry back in the 1970s had modeled itself on a human health model that, as we all know, is seriously broken. As a result, it created products that didn't provide value or allow the industry to gain in purpose, stature, or economic surety. And its reputation for being customer-friendly was frightfully bad.

This presented someone, somewhere, with the opportunity to succeed and change the course of an entire industry, if only they had access to the right model, culture and execution—like Chris and Natasha Ashton.

*

America's love affair with pets becomes more extreme by the day. Pets are the new American kids! We look at pets very differently now than we did even ten years ago. If it costs $8,000 to keep your dog alive and thriving, many families will choose to spend the money. And veterinary practice has reached the point where it's almost equal to human practice and cost.

Pet insurance was invented in the UK. And Petplan UK, which opened its doors in the mid-1970s, is the largest pet health insurer in the world. One-third of pets in Britain have health insurance; in America, less than 1 percent of our 175 million dogs and cats are so protected.

In Philadelphia, Pennsylvania, we've created Petplan USA, a tremendous, fast-growing, top-rated company that will protect our customers' beloved pets and create great wealth and opportunity for our team members and shareholders.

The story of Petplan in the US started, as many new businesses do, with an unexpected crisis. It became a true American success story.

Chris and Natasha Ashton were MBA candidates at my alma mater, Wharton School of Business at the University of Pennsylvania. They moved to Philadelphia in 2001 from their native Britain with four suitcases and a Birman cat named Bodey. Barely a month into their studies, the cat became quite ill.

Five thousand dollars in veterinary expenses later, they started looking into pet insurance and were distressed by the extremely limited choices compared with what they had in the UK. A family emergency blossomed into their passion.

The Ashtons, who met at Oxford University, came to Wharton because they wanted to set up a maritime, anti-piracy security business together, one that leveraged Chris's military security experience after seven years as a Royal Marine Commando and Natasha's background in shipping.

But as they painfully paid that vet bill and moved into less costly living quarters to cut expenses, the Ashtons had a fresh moment of inspiration: Americans needed a new and improved model if pet insurance was to ever catch fire in the US.

"We thought we could leverage our knowledge of pet insurance in the UK and introduce a product that provides a type of coverage that the American market hadn't seen before," Natasha said. "We wanted to reinvent and redefine American pet insurance."

It quickly became apparent that it was an enormous business opportunity, even during the economic downturn then gripping the country. Pet products, it turns out, are generally recession-proof.

It was a great idea, but they had no capital to start a national business in an unfamiliar land—indebted as they already were thanks to $250,000 in student loan debt.

The Ashtons quickly realized that Americans' pet obsession runs just as deep as—*or deeper* than!—that of Europeans when they saw that pets are a bigger industry than toys or candy. (In 2012 alone, Americans were projected to spend more than

$60 billion on their pets. Per head, Americans spend more on pets than folk do in Europe.)

The Ashtons refined a business plan that for the first time provided real value to American pet owners. They learned that, according to Datamonitor (2008), one in every three pets requires unexpected veterinary care each year. In addition, 40 percent of all claims received by Petplan are for chronic conditions that last beyond 12 months. These statistics show that health insurance for pets has become a financial necessity, not a luxury. Dramatic advances in veterinary medicines have provided pet owners with new treatment options, but these can be expensive. In 2009–10, American pet owners spent $12.2 billion on veterinary care, and that number is expected to rise.

Pet insurance can be an invaluable tool for pet owners as it allows for the best care, but it also prevents them from having to make difficult decisions regarding their pets' health. The financial burden that pet owners may face should a beloved pet become seriously ill or injured can be alleviated through insurance, which can help provide life-saving treatment. Ultimately, pet insurance is a smart way for pet owners to be forward thinking in protecting the health of these beloved family members and perhaps, more importantly, preserve their own peace of mind by minimizing the financial burden that can come from unexpected health crises.

Consider this: there are more than 500 inherited diseases in purebred dogs and more than 300 in mixed-breed dogs. At the time of the Ashtons' inquiry, no American pet insurer was providing coverage for those kinds of treatment. And yet those were precisely the costs people were looking to protect themselves against. Under existing American pet policies, the Ashtons would have been reimbursed just $500 on their cat's $5,000 vet bill, which didn't make any sense.

Petplan UK, the world's largest pet insurance provider, based just outside London, granted the Ashtons an exclusive license in the US and gave them access to 30 years' worth of proprietary actuarial pet data, experience, and know-how, which enabled them to create the products that were revolutionary in the marketplace.

They sold their first policy in July 2006. Two years later, Petplan was licensed in all 50 states.

In its first five years of operation, in one of the most challenging economic climates the world had seen in a long time, Petplan experienced tremendous growth, rising to number 123 in *Inc.* magazine's list of the 500 Fastest Growing Companies in America in 2011.

For a premium of $300–400 per year, customers receive an annual coverage limit of $10,000–20,000 a year and the pet is covered for life.

Petplan now has 100,000 pets insured in the US and, while that is an enormous number for a start-up—as is the 40 percent annual growth rate—it's just a fraction of the uninsured dogs and cats across the nation. There is a phenomenal need and opportunity to act. When the Ashtons have insured just 1 percent of the pets in America, the value of the company will be $1 billion.

*

Petplan USA is an example of building a serious new company from scratch by actually exceeding the New Math described in Chapter 5:

Model + Culture + Execution = Fans
Protect the brand (do nothing stupid!)
Refine the brand (make it better all the time!)
Expand the brand (find new products and new areas
where we can add value!)

At Petplan, there are many things that set us apart from our competitors. First and foremost is our approach to the business as a whole. We conceived this company as a pet health business first and foremost and secondarily as an insurance company. This approach really underpins everything we do because we are strictly focused on pet health. Pets come first, and this led us to create policies that are far more comprehensive than any competitor's.

We provide simple, straightforward policies with no exclusions, relatively speaking.

Being a pet company, not an insurance company, is a real distinction for us and it helps to create fans because no one enjoys buying insurance. We're more focused on being pet people and being a pet company. That's how we create the passion that is essential to build our brand.

Our model is that of a premium service, not a cheap, low-value product.

Chris and Natasha started Petplan USA with an engaging, clearly defined brand that set it apart from the competition. I later challenged them to aggressively pursue partnerships and to open up more channels on a nationwide and international basis. We have already expanded into Canada and that is only the beginning.

When I joined Petplan as chairman, the company was only open from 9 to 5, five days a week. I looked at Chris and Natasha and said, "That's ridiculous. Why aren't you open later during the week and second, why aren't you open on Saturdays and Sundays? Our banks are open seven days a week. Don't pet families want the same convenience and flexibility?" We extended our opening hours, making assistance available earlier and later than any other pet insurance company.

It comes down to service. We're a service company, whether that service is banking or pet health. When people call Petplan, they are often emotional, they're upset, their pet is sick and it's like a family member is ill. They need to talk to someone who will be empathetic, not hiding behind a website interface.

*

Petplan's success is aided by the nature of its main competitor, which has a complicated policy and schedule of benefits. Claimants are paid so much for this, so much for that, and the insurer spends its waking hours fighting *not* to pay valid claims. Many vets and customers dislike it immensely. At Petplan, customers submit their vet bill, we review it, subtract a deductible, and pay the balance.

Our main competitor does not cover hereditary diseases. But at least half of pet health problems today are hereditary diseases! Every breed has them, even mixed breeds.

And finally, most other companies won't accept pets as new enrollments after a certain age—typically 8–10 years old—the age at which most pets, like people, begin to break down.

All of these are anti-customer gimmicks. We do just the opposite. We kill every stupid rule so there's a clear differentiation between what we offer as a product—*model + culture + execution = FANS not customers*—and what the competition sells.

*

I met the Ashtons through our family's involvement at the University of Pennsylvania's School of Veterinary Medicine. I bought into their vision and came on board as chairman in 2008, making a serious investment in the company.

Shirley and I liked the idea of working with an up-and-coming, husband-and-wife management team. We saw a lot of ourselves in Chris and Natasha—not to mention our shared love of pets. A business mentoring relationship developed quite naturally, and we're proud of our association with Petplan and its adoption of many Metro Bank principles.

Chris and Natasha began refining their business model by adopting many of our proven business principles. Petplan is succeeding by focusing on the *FANS not customers* New Math:

- **Differentiated model.** By insuring hereditary diseases, paying vet bills without a claims schedule, and focusing on pets, not insurance, the company reinvented and redefined the market.
- **Unique culture.** With Petplan's institutionalized love of pets and a total service culture, the company reinforces its model.
- **Fanatical execution.** We get happy customers, 100 percent of the time—and a remarkable 80-plus percent renewal rate.

The result is fans not customers:

- 5–7% market share, number one American pet insurer
- 50 percent compound growth rate
- 80 percent policy renewals.

*

One of the other things I've tried to instill in the Ashtons is that they have to be visible spokespersons for their brand—the "Pied Pipers" of Petplan.

"That was a bit alien to us, but now we see it," Chris said. "It's essential that the business has a personality behind it, and here, that's the two of us."

They learned the secrets of American-style business networking, constantly telling their company's story to everyone they met.

Another area of emphasis on which I have worked with the Ashtons is speed of decision-making. When we met, they overanalyzed everything, often to the point of business paralysis. They like to not make mistakes, but in business, you've got to make a decision and confidently move ahead. Nobody knows every time which decisions will work and which won't. But you'll never know if you don't choose.

"If anything, we learned that inaction will kill the business," Natasha said. "You'd be better off making the decision and correcting all the way than just doing nothing."

*

One of the first things that the Ashtons and I agreed upon in joining forces on Petplan was that to build a culture, we must hire for attitude and train for skill. If we hire people who are passionate about pets and who empathize with our policyholders, that practice will set us up for the best types of experiences.

Recruiting is a behavior. We can teach technical skills, but our culture, when it focuses on customer services, is the ability to be *nice*—the ability to smile all the time, to exceed expectations.

The lion's share of these things is innate, and that's what our culture is built around because it's our differentiator. Knowing, understanding, and matching our culture to our business model, and hiring the right people and training them the right way is the key to success in any business. We may just believe in it more strongly than other companies.

Just as important to maintaining a great culture is recognizing when we make a mistake by hiring someone who doesn't absorb and apply our unique culture. If a person doesn't fit within our culture, and cannot execute our model, perhaps Petplan is not the right place for them.

*

At Petplan, the *FANS not customers* approach underpins everything we do.

It's not just a question of meeting customers' expectations. Every day, we look for ways to go above and beyond, from planting a tree in memory of their dog or cat when it passes away to hand-delivering policies if we need to support a customer in an extraordinary situation.

Everyone in the company will go out of their way to make sure that our policyholders continue receiving the kind of service and support that will make them tell their family and friends about us.

At Petplan, our customer call center is often the company's primary contact with policyholders. This is where we build and earn fans not customers.

We have a three-week training program in place, but every person we hire *must* be passionate about pets, must be a pet lover first and foremost, because otherwise they couldn't possibly begin to empathize with the owner of a sick or injured dog or cat.

We ask them, "Do you have pets?," and we can tell immediately what kind of pet owner they are. We talk about their pets and how they feel about their pets and what kind of experience they've had when their pets are sick. We ask, "How did that make you feel?," and "How was your experience with the veterinarian?" That's how we determine whether they're going to be able to guide our policyholders through traumatic events when their pets are sick.

Most of a policyholder's experience with the Petplan call center happens off script because we want our team members to empathize with the policyholder. It's more of a question of having tools that they can use. When someone calls up and says they have a Cavalier King Charles spaniel, they can immediately say, "Oh, our founders have one of those! They're great dogs, very affectionate, but did you know they suffer from congenital heart conditions?"

Our happiness managers on the service side form deep bonds with policyholders. In one case, a manager learned that a Petplan policyholder was going through cancer treatment at the same time as her dog. She called up fairly regularly as she struggled to deal with her own illness and her pet's at the same time. The same manager always took the woman's call, always spent as much time as needed to console the customer, comfort her, and one day she even sent her a big bouquet of flowers.

We're always looking for ways to connect; these really are genuine relationships. You can ask any of our happiness managers—a lot of them will refer to policyholders as friends.

We came to realize fairly early on that by virtue of the nature of our business, many of the pets we insure will at some point pass away, and we lose many pets over the policy year. A company we support will plant a tree in the pet's name and then send a note to the policyholder to let them know that we've commemorated their pet.

Couple those relationships with all the things that we do very, very well—cash management, extended hours, no stupid rules—and we wind up with *FANS not customers* across all our business lines.

*

Marketing is an area in which that couldn't possibly be truer.

"Design is a competitive advantage and we have really focused on the design of everything that Petplan does," Chris says, "from the office itself all the way through collateral marketing materials such as our magazine and website. Everything we do is highly designed. We rely on photography to reach out and touch people and that has really worked in our favor. It's something that Commerce Bank was about from the get-go."

Petplan doesn't have stores like Metro Bank does. But that's *precisely* why design is a competitive weapon in its business as well. Because pet insurance is an intangible product, design is paramount. We focused on creating a pet-friendly brand, and design underpins everything we do.

The product that a customer buys from us is a policy. And most pet insurance policies are black-and-white, 8.5 × 11 inch pieces of paper with just the details printed on them because that's the easiest way to do it. Our marketing team designed beautiful policy documents that are now sent electronically—saving printing and shipping costs—with color throughout. Pet families don't expect this in their first interaction with us. These well-crafted documents tie in with the Petplan website (www.gopetplan.com) and also our call center.

Our Petplan offices are also beautifully designed because they are part of the culture, part of our brand. The offices don't resemble those of a typical insurance company. There are bright yellow walls with dog bowls hanging on them. There's amazing photography of America's beloved pets everywhere you walk. From the beginning we felt that photography would engage our potential customers, so we recruited the services of one of the country's leading pet photographers. She has taken thousands of photos of our policyholders' pets which we then use across our marketing materials.

We introduced the first-ever pet health magazine, *fetch!*, free for all our policyholders.

When we first launched *fetch!*, there was a significant start-up cost. It's not a cheap publication, certainly when you consider the element of design and the high quality of the paper that we use. Early on it cost us more to produce than pretty much anything else, but we couldn't put a price tag on what it did for our relationship with policyholders and our renewal rates. Now the magazine pays for itself through advertising, but right from the start, I didn't object to spending the money because it's about long-term relationship building.

Sometimes, if you're focused so much on cost, you miss the bigger picture.

fetch! has become so popular that it now has a paid subscriber base. It is sold nationwide through Barnes & Noble and continues to gain in popularity. It's one of the most widely read pet publications in America.

We also created a pet health blog. Our website is focused on

animal health, so from policy design all the way to our interaction with the consumer, everything we do focuses on pet
health as opposed to just the transaction of insurance.

Through this attention to design—on top of our customer-
centric service and commitment to pet owners—we have made
our mark on the industry and clearly differentiated Petplan from
the competition. Every touch point with the customer is beautiful to behold. The website is clean, it's easy to use.

Whether you're walking into the Petplan office, reading
fetch!, picking up one of our brochures, surfing the website or
receiving our newsletter, you know it's Petplan. You can't miss
the quality.

*

Petplan USA has been another great example of creating wealth
by adding customer value through a unique, differentiated
model, a persuasive culture supporting the model, and the right
financial execution.

This is a true American success story that you can emulate
in your own business.

16

Closing Words from a Man Who Never Closes Shop

To be a benevolent organization, you have to make a lot of profit. But if your sole goal is to maximize profit, you're on a collision course with time. We've made commitments that have become accretive to the brand, but it was never by design.

Howard Schultz, chairman, Starbucks

My father, who sold his business and retired in 1992, was proud of my success with Commerce Bank.

When he died a few years later, the bank had assets of $4 billion. To him, it was a tremendous success. But his attitude was, "Well, that's over with, what will you do next?" And rather than be insulted by that as some might be, I felt the same way. We have a company line: "We got paid for last year's success already, what are we doing now?"

The banking industry naysayers said, "Service and convenience are charming when you are small, but when you get bigger, you can't do it." And haven't we proven everybody wrong about that!

Size breeds momentum! But it can also breed complacency. This model of ours is about getting into people's heads, hearts, minds, and souls, and then letting them do their jobs. We don't micromanage. Our environment, our culture, and our management style are not about that. Every time we went outside and hired someone, we worried that we would lose our culture. We went to great pains—and we still do—to de-program new people joining us, to AMAZE them and get them to see that ours really is a better way.

Great businesses create fans by redefining or creating industries through unique combinations of the model + culture + execution formula. By creating great brands they then create value, which benefits everyone from the fans to the shareholders.

Anyone who has created a true growth company has been an agent of change by creating a new industry; reinventing an existing industry; going against conventional wisdom; enduring the barbs of the competition, media, and a skeptical public; and thinking completely outside the box.

When Bill Gates founded Microsoft he believed in the PC, but at the time conventional wisdom favored the mainframe. IBM missed the chance to buy Microsoft because it did not understand the new world that it essentially inspired. Facing enormous competition, government obstruction, and public doubt, the kid from Seattle empowered the world while changing conventional wisdom.

Ray Kroc saw the magic of fast food through the milkshake machine. He understood that Americans wanted quality, speed, and consistency. With little competition, McDonald's swept the world, making obsolete existing models that could not change with the times.

Warren Buffett turned an almost bankrupt shirt maker into an industry powerhouse by harnessing—from Omaha, Nebraska, of all places—the power of insurance premium floats and value investing.

During the Commerce journey, we were attacked and opposed by the Old Guard competition, regulators, and skeptics.

In the beginning, of course, we were too small to matter. Then the competition said a service-focused model could never work. Soon, they said we were only getting the accounts nobody wanted!

In the mid-1990s, the conventional wisdom was that the internet would replace the branch banking system. We believed—against the grain—that the customer wanted the best of every delivery channel and we continued to offer both. And in 2001, we chose to invade Manhattan despite a chorus of emboldened skeptics. How could our banking model be superior to the entrenched competition?

Our answer? How could:

- Bill Gates outflank IBM?
- Sam Walton bankrupt Kmart?
- Howard Schultz reinvent coffee?
- Steve Jobs re-imagine mobile phones?

All of us reached for common themes:

- A value-added differentiated MODEL
- A pervasive, unique CULTURE
- A fanatical EXECUTION

All of us succeeded in creating *FANS not customers.*

*

My job, whether at Metro Bank or Petplan, is to protect the brand, to define the brand, and to expand the brand. And to that end, I have five basic responsibilities every day of my working life:

- **Develop** the model
- **Install** the model
- **Instill** the model

- **Enforce** the model
- **Improve** the model

Our business model is to attack the competition, their stupid rules and wrong-headed traditions—attack on the ground, attack in the air, attack in the press.

We have a saying at Metro Bank: "To err is human; to recover is Metro." We will make errors, whether at Metro Bank or Petplan, but how we recover from the error is going to determine whether you are a fan, not a customer.

Our people are told, "We only have a few rules, but you are empowered to overrule them."

That's the opposite of the message that every other bank employee gets at every other bank.

Even Betty Crocker will burn a cake every once in a while. We will make mistakes. We process millions of transactions a month. Somewhere there will be an error. Take ownership of the problem, fix the problem, and fix the mess that was created by the problem. If we make a mistake and don't post a deposit and related cheques bounce, we'll fix the problem by giving the customer the proper credit for the deposit. But we'll go beyond that. We'll contact all the affected parties, including the payees on the cheques that bounced. If they need letters or phone calls, whatever it takes, fix the problem, but also fix the mess that you may have caused.

Recovery takes many forms:

- **Step 1: Take ownership of the problem.** For a moment, be on the customer's side. Take care of it, even if it's a problem the customer caused. When things go wrong, there's almost an instinctive urge to direct the customer's attention elsewhere. Don't do it. The buck stops with us.

- **Step 2: Listen to find the problem.** The importance of good listening cannot be overstated. In a problem-solving situation, we are listening for two reasons: to allow the customer to vent their frustration; and to find the real problem (which may be obvious, but sometimes isn't).

- **Step 3: Clarify and clearly understand the problem, and repeat it back to the customer.** Make it clear that *we* agree that what the customer sees really is a problem.

- **Step 4: Solve the customer's problem.** If the problem is one that we have encountered before, we may already know the best solution. If we need help, we get it. Maybe we can't fix it in front of the customer. Tell them that we'll fix it, when, and get back to them to confirm resolution. By involving customers in generating the solution it will start to rebuild the relationship. Most customers usually bring a sense of fair play and will often expect far less than we'd think.

- **Step 5: The satisfaction guarantee.** Now we go the extra mile, utilizing our "Satisfaction Guarantee Program." This offers a value-added gesture that says, "We want to make it up to you."

Beyond these steps, if we can't fix the basic problem, we try and take care of the mess it caused. For example, if the customer's cheque bounced through no fault of ours, why not try to help the customer resolve their problem?

Recovery is an art. And in most cases, every customer problem represents an opportunity to win a customer for life. People make mistakes all the time, and we don't hang them out to dry for making a mistake. We try to educate them. There is no mistake that we can't fix, so we tell team members not to torture themselves over it. We tell them, "If you screw up, let us know."

If there is a written complaint, people usually say, "I expect a response; don't palm me off to lower level management." We always touch those customers. It could be a cheque account problem, and when we resolve it, we might add £50 to their account as an apology for making the mistake.

When we recognize we've made a mistake, we contact the customer. We have satisfaction rewards worth £20 apiece, and a Metro Bank executive will sometimes write a letter saying, "So-and-So will call you to resolve your issue. In the meantime, I am depositing £100 in your account to make up for the mistake." We don't want a customer to leave and bad-mouth us to ten friends. Regardless of the amount a customer has in their account, they will get the attention of a regional vice president, a market manager, or a senior retail market manager. We protect the brand; that's really what it's about.

We take ownership of every customer's problem—and solve it. The buck stops with our team member. If they can't solve the basic problem, they will take care of any inconveniences it causes. Then they help us deliver AMAZE!ing service by asking a manager or supervisor for a satisfaction guarantee cheque that they can present to the customer who encountered the snag.

We want our customers to know we're dedicated to providing them with AMAZE!ing service at all times.

Ninety-nine percent of the complaints that reach me personally are a result of somebody not waiving a rule at the first level—that is, somebody enforcing a rule that they should have waived.

Use inevitable failures in your business to create even more fans.

*

Creating a true growth business means taking a special journey in which you will go against the grain, exposing yourself to failure, ridicule, disappointment, and, if you are lucky, success.

Risk takers sometimes succeed. Many die on the trail. The more success you have, the more the critics will attack. You, your model, and your culture need to be strong to survive and strong enough to evolve when the time comes.

As Metro Bank has grown from a one-office bank to a fast-growing regional lender, we have faced and will continue to face unending challenges from every direction.

If yours is a market share *take* model—as ours is—you can expect competition to defend and attack by every method. Be prepared—and be confident.

*

These are the essential lessons that I hope you will take away from this book:

- The brand is who you are, what you are, and what your customers expect!
- Hope is not a plan.
- No one needs a "Me, Too" anything.
- Differentiate. Improve. Strive.
- You can try to cost-cut your way to prosperity, or you can grow your way to prosperity. (*We believe in the latter.*)
- Value creators are wealth creators.
- Shareholders are your boss, your fellow team members—YOU!
- Stock options make every team member an *owner*.
- Ordinary companies are great at counting the parts, but have no concept of the value of a whole. Companies with fans value the whole experience.

My journey has exceeded my expectations. Our customers have become our fans and propelled us to undreamed of success. Our combination of value differentiated model, unique and pervasive culture, and fanatical execution will continue to create fans.

You can do the same. Remember to:

- define success in your own terms;
- find your particular talent;
- create a business or career model that reflects your dreams;
- prepare yourself for success;
- then just do it.

We believe the best is yet to come at Metro Bank and Petplan and wish you good luck on *your* journey!

What they say about Vernon Hill

Tom Brown
Founder, BankStocks.com
In 1998, I was reading the *Wall Street Journal,* and there was this front page story about a bank that I had never heard of in New Jersey and how successful they were and how different they were from everybody else, because they were opening branches like crazy when everybody else was closing them.

It was Commerce Bank.

They didn't care if the customers had different levels of profitability and that some customers were unprofitable, they served everybody equally. They offered extended hours in their branches, their cost of doing business was high, when the rest of the banks that I was looking at were lowering their cost of delivery, so everything that I thought was going to lead to being a winner, Commerce was doing just the opposite.

I was at Tiger Management at the time, and I called up the bank and asked to speak to the CEO. Much to my surprise, not now but then, Vernon Hill took the call. We spent maybe an hour and a half on the phone. He was telling me about the bank and concluded with, "You really should come down here and see us." Soon I met with him in his office, and he said, "Let's go out and visit some of these stores." That was an eye-opening experience for me, and it really changed the way I looked at what it was going to take to be successful in retail banking. In fact, a lot of what I thought banks would be able to execute, they weren't able to do. It was too complicated. Systems didn't talk to each other. Meanwhile, Commerce was knocking the cover off the ball.

One of the things that I enjoy is a good spar. Vernon does, too, so it was a match made in heaven between the two of us. We had a great discussion.

What was incredibly unusual was that the CEO would drive me around to individual branches. The CEOs at most of the companies that I looked at didn't even know where their branches were. Another CEO would never know anybody inside that branch, so all of this was different. The other thing that he did was point out competitor branches along the way.

Most of the CEOs of big banks do not come from the retail side of the business. Most came from the corporate side of business, so there was, until 2000, inattention to the retail side.

In banking, there is certainly an over-emphasis on not failing. Don't do something different if you might fail at it. Vernon has not been afraid. One of the most important elements of his success is that he has not been afraid to try things that either nobody else does or that conventional wisdom says is wrong.

At our firm, we do what is called an annual "Branch Hunt." That's where we divide up into teams, and we walk down each of the avenues on the East Side of Manhattan. Everybody is given about $500, and they are told that they have to open two current accounts at two different institutions. They check out every financial institution. If they don't open two current accounts, they give the money back, and nobody has ever given me any money back. At the end of the branch hunt, we all get together and tell our stories and show our pictures, and that was when it became hilarious how poor the execution of everybody else was compared with Commerce. There was this woman that helped us at Commerce. I said, "How did you find Commerce?" She said, "I moved here from South America, and I was working for a dentist. I asked the dentist, 'Where should I open a checking account?' He said, 'Commerce Bank, because they work late hours, and they are open late, and it would be very convenient.'" So she opened up her current account there, and she was so impressed with the people that she quit her job as a dental assistant and went to work for Commerce Bank.

I think Shirley, Vernon's wife, was the secret weapon of Commerce Bank and is exactly that now at Metro Bank. She is the keeper of the brand, produces design as a competitive weapon, and enforces the culture.

I was in Atlanta and one of my meetings was at SunTrust, which is one of the top ten banks in the US. I was listening to them talk about how they're changing their approach to retail and it got me thinking about the old Commerce model. The thing about the old Commerce model that, frankly, Vernon and I disagreed with each other on was that if I asked him "What's the key to the system?", he would say, "The system!" I would say it was the branch manager and I still felt that when I was listening to how SunTrust was redefining the job of the branch manager; then I thought of the branch managers that participated in the old Commerce system.

They were disproportionately women. They were anywhere from 35 to 60 years of age and the big difference between them and their competitors was, number one, that the women *owned* their branch. They'd do the branch's deposit totals and they were the number one small business banker for that branch. By the way, these women—mostly women, there were some men— were happy being a branch manager and they weren't viewing it as a stepping-stone. You literally could go across the street to a PNC branch or what's now a Wells Fargo branch and you'd see a 20-something-year-old male running the branch and they wouldn't want to be there. They were doing this, they hoped, for two years and then they'd be on to something else.

The women managers, on the other hand, liked the flexibility of hours, the fact it was close to home, that they were serving their friends. Most of the branch managers in the Commerce system were very local. You wouldn't necessarily find that in the biggest banks.

It was fun when Vernon would take me in his car and we'd go to Commerce branches and we'd go to competitors and what was striking was who these people were at his branches and how they knew their numbers and how *Vernon* knew their numbers. There were very few metrics that they focused on, so the key metric was, "What are my deposits?"

And then we'd go by the competitors' branches and notice how the larger competitors got their branches primarily through acquisition as opposed to construction. I remember one where I couldn't even tell it was a Wachovia branch.

Vernon reinvented American retail banking. His focus on service created a true growth retailer. No one else has grown an American bank internally at 25 percent per year for 30-plus years. *No one.*

Meredith Whitney
Founder, Meredith Whitney Advisory Group, LLC
Before launching my own consulting firm, I was a bank analyst for CIBC. March 17, 2005, was the first time I went down to Cherry Hill, New Jersey, to meet the chairman of Commerce Bank, Vernon Hill. I was preparing to initiate coverage on Commerce.

I had heard a lot about them. Commerce was a controversial stock, high-flying in terms of being a well-performing stock, but there was a lot of controversy around management. Any time you see a stock go up so far so fast, there will be controversy.

Banks can make themselves as complicated as they want. Commerce was not complicated, and that is why I was so comfortable recommending it.

I initiated coverage on June 1, 2005, which was the low point of the stock for the year. I had such a fortuitous opportunity to recommend the stock then, but I was trying to see what I was missing, because people I knew were so negative about the Commerce name. From my vantage point, the bank's story was so simple: focus on customer service, which is a revolutionary concept for banks, and give customers the simplest product with high touch, high service.

How they made money was simple. They didn't put a lot of credit risk on the balance sheet.

This was the least controversial stock I would ever cover. That's from a fundamental standpoint.

I liked Commerce for reasons that most bank analysts should have liked Commerce. I think that Vernon Hill always likes to tell the story of Commerce as a retail investment, but I looked at Commerce as a *bank* investment.

If you walked around in New York City during the early 2000s, there were lines out the door of Commerce stores. People went nuts for Commerce. I think that, for a lot of people in New York and areas where Commerce was, it was such a different experience. They certainly revolutionized the idea of consumer banking in the minds of many people.

I was at the opening of the first branch of Metro Bank in London. It was incredible. Incredible! It's Commerce—and even better.

Vernon rarely looks back and is almost solely focused on how he can create business opportunities today. He is the most growth-oriented guy that I can think of. When he meets someone, it's always, "How can we do business together?" He wastes no time trying to figure out what is the best business scenario for two people, or how they can both be beneficial to each other. He's great. He's just extraordinarily efficient, and that tells the story of his success again and again and again.

William C. Taylor
Co-founder, Fast Company *magazine, and author,* Mavericks At Work

Commerce Bank stood out when I was doing research for my book *Mavericks At Work* because what they were doing was so rare and virtually nonexistent in the banking business.

Something Vernon said to me, which has stuck with me, is that "Every great company has re-imagined the industry that it's in."

I think if you look at the Commerce Bank story, they rethought and re-imagined the sense of what was possible in the financial services business. First, what could it mean to be a bank? Psychologically and emotionally, what could the experience for a customer be encountering an institution which is part of the day-to-day fabric of life after all? Second, from the point of view of the strategy with which you compete in the business, the business model with which you go to market, could you rethink and re-imagine a lot of the traditional logic of how banks make money, what banks think are important in terms of the deposits they're gathering and the loans they're making or whatever the case may be?

And so what really struck me about Commerce Bank more than anything was that there was an ironclad connection with the economic value proposition. That is to say the strategy and the costs and the ways of operating around which the business was built, and the human values proposition, the culture, the experience, the design, and the sensibility that customers encountered day-to-day doing business.

I think that magical connection between economic value and human values is really, in some sense, what informs most really great companies and most really great brands—we certainly see it with Apple in computing. We see it with Four Seasons in hospitality, and who would think we would see it in the banking world as well?

That's what really made me sit up and take notice of Commerce Bank.

A lot of what I do is look at very successful organizations and the strategy they use to create economic value, and the culture and approach to innovation they use to compete on human values. It strikes me that for many, many years of their long run, there was such clarity in the minds of Vernon, his senior team and the rank and file organization: *This is the game we're playing. This is how we're changing the game in our business. This is the kind of culture and human commitment we need to make sure that as we succeed and get bigger we don't lose sight of the fact of those things that made us successful in the first place.*

And there was such a design mindset, not just about what the stores looked like or what their colors were, but also about the business strategy, the expansion strategy, the physical design of the stores, and the social design of the culture. That means that the business became scalable and sustainable.

What strikes me about so many organizations that start fast with a great idea is that eventually they run out of steam because success has a funny way of sowing the seeds of a demise. Can you maintain the same level of urgency and commitment and passion and creativity with 5,000 employees as you did with 50? It's one thing to have some good financial results when the big boys aren't paying any attention to you, but once you get to a size where people are starting to pay attention and the competitive backlash begins, are you able to withstand that competitive backlash?

What impressed me so much about the rise of Commerce Bank to become such a big player is that as it got bigger, the culture remained consistent, the performance remained elevated, and the business strategy continued to hold its own, even as they were going up against some of the biggest banks in the world—and that's another part of the story that really impressed me.

There is such tunnel vision among the big incumbent players in just about every business. It's as if CEO Moses handed down the tablets about "This is what it means to be a bank. This is what it means to be an airline. This is what it means to be a hospital." There's a standard issue strategic mindset. There are all kinds of standard operating procedures and most incumbents are perfectly content to kind of nip and tuck in the margins and, "Hey we'll be 3 percent cheaper in this product line and we'll try to have our employees be 5 percent more responsive in this service area," and everybody plays the same game. Then you try to be incrementally better than the next guy. Everybody is pretty good at everything.

Then you come across an organization like Commerce that was absolutely the most of something. The most intensely focused on the customer experience; the most intensely focused on gathering deposits as the economic fuel that keeps the engine going. The big established players—and this is not just true of banks, it's true about everything—look at what seems like an alien life force, a kind of outlier to the standard model of the business, and they really don't know what to make of it. They have no capacity to mimic it. It gets bigger and bigger and attracts their attention, so what do they do? They may try to copy a few of the surface innovations. "Okay, we'll stay open a little longer." Or, "We'll put a few coin counting machines in our high-traffic locations." They copy a few of the particular innovations, and yet they don't ever seem to pay any dividends in terms of economic performance because all they're doing is taking on a bunch of the extra costs that a bank like Commerce did, but they're unable to deliver the whole experience so they get none of the benefits.

Vernon told me that the whole point is that it's a *symphony*. The performance works because everything works in concert, so if you don't buy it in its entirety, you can't ever get it to work for you. Vernon's competition over the years simply refused to learn from Commerce.

The classic example of this, outside banking, was in the airline industry where you had the rise of Southwest and JetBlue. Then Delta created Song and United launched Ted. Both tried kind of reluctantly, kind of half-heartedly, to say, "We'll have our version of JetBlue," which was Song for Delta. And "We'll have our version of Southwest," which was Ted for United. And "We'll try to be a little quirky and we'll fly the same 737 plane that Southwest flies and we'll try to turn the planes around in 25 minutes rather than an hour and five minutes." They could never get it to work because they were copying the surface innovations or mimicking the tangible performance, but they didn't have the culture to do it. They didn't have the sense of camaraderie.

Southwest can turn around its planes quickly because everybody works together, including the pilots. If you've got unions that are at odds with one another and unions that are at odds with the company, you can't make all that stuff happen. Two or three years into it United and Delta were completely shocked at how hard it was and they put both Song and Ted out of business. And so it goes in every industry. Incumbent players with an ingrained mindset find it very hard to learn from, let alone mimic, the strategies and practices and culture of a genuine outside-the-box innovator. I see this everywhere, so I'm not that surprised that the big banks (a) never took Commerce seriously, and (b) were never able to figure out how to respond to it because it's outside the established repertoire, basically.

Everybody says "Seeing is believing," but as Steve Jobs said, "Believing is seeing."

Appendix: Lingo

Successful businesses almost always have unique keywords and phrases that are used internally to describe a culture, or help them build the model. In this final section, we're pulling back the curtain a little further to reveal a few more concepts and programs that make Metro Bank an industry innovator.

AMAZE!	Our customers' perception of Metro Bank when we deliver service experiences that exceed their expectations
AMAZE! Answer Guide	A searchable keyword index on Lotus Notes that can help you immediately answer any questions a customer asks. It's the answer to every question a customer can ask, updated every day on every computer
AMAZE! Awards	A high-energy, large-scale annual awards ceremony held to reward team members who have demonstrated superior customer service throughout the year

AMAZE! Patrol	A group of Metro Bank team members, carrying balloons, prizes and other goodies, who make surprise visits to team members who have earned WOW! recognition
AMAZE! Spotlight	A popular quarterly publication that highlights members of the Metro Bank team who are "doing it right" and salutes their great performances
AMAZE! Van	The bright blue Metro Bank mini vans which are painted with Metro's "AMAZE! the Customer" logo on all sides, used to transport Metro Man, and often parked in high visibility areas during special events
AMAZE! Wiz	A support team superstar who currently is being recognized for his or her AMAZE! efforts during the quarter and is featured prominently on the nearest "Wall of AMAZE!"
Brand	Who we are, what we are and what the customers expect! The distinct identities Metro Bank and Petplan USA have created for themselves through their unique approach to the services business and the delivery of uncommon convenience and unparalleled, legendary customer service
Bump it up	To resolve a customer's dilemma by contacting a supervisor or manager in order to obtain immediate answers to the customer's questions

Buzz/buzzing	The excitement generated when Metro Bank team members WOW! their customers
Competitors' Rules and Practices (CRAP)	The stuff that drives customers at other banks crazy. You know, the stuff that customers will never find at Metro Bank or Petplan
Customer	That's Customer with a capital "C"— the most important part of our lives at Metro Bank and Petplan. Customers rule!
Customers	Anyone who purchases Metro Bank or Petplan products or services through you—the people who pay our salaries
Customer experience	The compilation of everything that touches the sense of a customer when he or she comes into contact with Metro Bank and Petplan. The appearance of a workspace is a crucial element of the customer experience. The appearance of our team members (the way they dress, their tone of voice, their body language), the product presentation, and the overall delivery of service are other essential aspects of the customer experience
FANS	What all our customers should become by feeling so satisfied about the AMAZE! service we provide that they talk passionately about Metro as "my bank," "my investment firm," or "my insurance company." Also applies to "my insurance company, Petplan"

Growth	An essential force that fuels Metro's current and future success by producing dramatic increases in customers, deposits, loans, and shareholder value; ditto for Petplan with regard to policyholders
How's Our Support	The program through which retail team members are given the opportunity to provide feedback to team members in support areas
Idea Bank	The program through which team members can send their ideas about improving Metro Bank and Petplan policies or procedures and earn a cash bonus for each idea that is implemented
Internal customer	Any Metro Bank or Petplan team member who depends on your support to provide an external customer with truly memorable service
"M" stickers	Little red stickers in the shape of the Metro Bank "M" logo, used by all managers and supervisors to reward team members who they catch "doing it right." "WOW!ers" who receive the stickers can redeem them for cool, exclusive merchandise

Magic Money Machine	Metro Bank's user-friendly, interactive coin counting machines located in every store, absolutely free to use by customers and non-customers—simply pour loose change into the machine and press "START." The Magic Money Machine prints a receipt that can be taken to a cashier in exchange for cash or a deposit into an account
Major AMAZE	The master of the AMAZE! philosophy. He periodically dispenses tips about the best ways to AMAZE! customers and reads through all team member letters about AMAZE! Award nominations and Idea Bank suggestions. He can always be reached through Lotus Notes
Metro Bank culture	The essence of who we are—the behaviors and beliefs of Metro Bank team members that come from an intense dedication to exceeding the expectations of customers and co-workers by delivering unsurpassed service to every customer, every day

- Say YES to Customers … One to say YES, Two to say NO!
- Make each Customer Feel Special!
- Always keep Customer Promises!
- Recover!! To err is human; to recover, Metro!
- Think like the Customer!

Metro Money Zone	Metro Bank's one-of-a-kind financial education program for kids in years 1–13, parents and teachers, designed to teach the importance of saving, as well as how to write a cheque, plan for a special purchase, invest in the stock market and much more. It includes in-class visits by Metro Bank team members, several special events and a wealth of online resources available through https://www.metrobankonline.co.uk/About-Us/KidsRock/
Metroize/metroized	The process of instilling in our team members the intense dedication and passion to providing superior customer service that Metro Bank has developed a reputation for delivering
Mr. M	Our official mascot in the shape of the Metro Bank "M" logo. It makes appearances at special events as a symbol of Metro
Mystery shopper	The program which employs "mystery shoppers" who visit or contact our team members in order to gauge the company's level of customer service
Non-customer	Someone who has not taken the opportunity to join the Metro Bank family by opening an account
One to Say YES, Two to Say NO	The rule that states all team members can say "Yes" to a customer, but they must check with their supervisor before saying "No"

Opportunity

What Metro Bank provides for team members and investors who want to be part of a rapidly growing company that offers exceptional career advancement and potential for financial growth

Petplan culture

The essence of who we are—the behaviors and beliefs of Petplan team members that come from an intense dedication to exceeding the expectations of customers and co-workers by delivering unsurpassed service to every customer, every day

Platform

The physical part of each store where customer service representatives serve customers

Red Friday

The celebration held in all Metro Bank offices every Friday, during which all team members wear red business attire (in honor of the color of the Metro logo) to reinforce our brand and energize customers and team members

Retailer

The mindset that differentiates Metro from all other banks. By thinking like the great power retailers of America (ie, McDonald's, Home Depot, Wal-Mart), Metro Bank provides customers with a truly different and better banking experience

Retailtainment

The art of engaging customers and creating moments of magic so that every customer leaves Metro Bank with a smile

Satisfaction guarantee cheque	To err is human; to recover is Metro. In addition to fixing any problems that may arise, we give customers £20 cheques as a token of our sincere apology
Shareholders	Your boss, your fellow team members—YOU!
Stupid rules	The Metro Bank program through which team members can earn £50 cash rewards for suggesting better alternatives to existing policies or procedures if their suggestions are implemented
Ten Minute Principle	A Metro Bank policy created to exceed customers' expectations by extending service to them ten minutes before our stores officially open and ten minutes after they officially close
Wall of AMAZE!	Display areas located throughout Metro Bank's operations facilities, featuring the names and photos of support team members who consistently WOW! customers, as well as those of team members celebrating service anniversaries during the current month
Warm transfer	The best way to handle customer calls that need to be directed to other Metro Bank team members. The process involves waiting for the next team member to answer the phone, explaining the customer's situation in full, and providing the customer with the new team member's name before putting the transfer through

Index